GETTING INTO POETRY

Also by Paul Hyland

POETRY

Riddles for Jack (Northern House, 1978)
Domingus (Mid-Day Publications, 1978)
Poems of Z (Bloodaxe Books, 1982)
The Stubborn Forest (Bloodaxe Books, 1984)
Kicking Sawdust (Bloodaxe Books, 1995)

TRAVEL & TOPOGRAPHY

Purbeck: The Ingrained Island (Gollancz, 1978; Dovecote, 1989)
Wight: Biography of an Island (Gollancz, 1984)
The Black Heart: A Voyage into Central Africa (Gollancz, 1988)
Indian Balm: Travels in the Southern Subcontinent
    (HarperCollins, 1994; Flamingo, 1995)
Backwards Out of the Big World (HarperCollins, 1996)

TRAVEL & TOPOGRAPHY

Babel Guide to the Fiction of Portugal, Brazil and Africa,
    with Ray Keeney & David Treece (Boulevard, 1995)

BLOODAXE POETRY
HANDBOOKS: 1

Paul Hyland

GETTING INTO POETRY

A READERS' & WRITERS' GUIDE TO THE POETRY SCENE

BLOODAXE BOOKS

Copyright © Paul Hyland & Bloodaxe Books 1992, 1996

ISBN: 1 85224 118 7

First published 1992 by
Bloodaxe Books Ltd,
P.O. Box 1SN,
Newcastle upon Tyne NE99 1SN.

Second edition 1996.

Bloodaxe Books Ltd acknowledges
the financial assistance of Northern Arts.

Cover printing by J. Thomson Colour Printers Ltd, Glasgow.

Printed in Great Britain by
Bell & Bain Limited, Glasgow, Scotland.

Contents

6   *Acknowledgements*

7   The Garret, the Ghetto and the Great Globe Itself

PART ONE: Taking It In

11   Sketch Map
30   Waterholes
35   Voices

PART TWO: Getting It Out

39   Riches
41   Winning Words
46   Put to Bed
57   Paranoia
61   Pundits and Gurus
66   Nice Little Earners
72   Allies
76   Toolkits, Workboxes
81   The Muse is not amused

PART THREE: Books & Sources

83   Landmarks
102   Listings

Acknowledgements

This book could not have been written without the help of poets, editors and arts officers who were willing to give time to answering my questions, making suggestions and dropping hints: Anna Adams, Gillian Allnutt, David Benedictus, Tony Bianchi, Vanessa Bone, Rachel Bourke, Christine Bridgwood, Richard Caddel, Walter Cairns, Laurence Cassidy, Gillian Clarke, Stewart Conn, Robert Crawford, Stuart Delves, Maura Dooley, Theo Dorgan, Peter Forbes, Harry Guest, Margaret Harlin, David Hart, John Harvey, Debbie Hicks, Jeremy Hooker, Richard Ings, Robert Johnstone, Andrew Lindesay, Hilary Llewellyn-Williams, Andrew McAllister, Máire Mhac an tSaoi, Mary Maher, Bob Mole, Peter Mortimer, Eiléan Ní Chuilleanáin, Harry Novak, Dennis O'Driscoll, Jilly Paver, Tessa Ransford, Peter Sansom, Jacqueline Simms, Matt Simpson, Iain Sinclair, Jane Spiers, Ingrid Squirrell, Martin Stannard, Julie Steele, Charmian Stowell, Simon Thirsk, John Wakeman, Maggie Ware and Emyr Williams. I am grateful to them all for their patience and generosity. Special thanks are due to Neil Astley for his encouragement from the very beginning, for his editorial tact and for the contribution he has made to the book, particularly the compilation of chapter 14. For permission to quote 'The Prize-Winning Poem' by Fleur Adcock, acknowledgements are due to the author and Oxford University Press.

CHAPTER ONE

The Garret, the Ghetto
and the Great Globe Itself

'If I read a book and it makes my whole body so cold no fire
can ever warm me, I know *that* is poetry. If I feel physically as
if the top of my head were taken off, I know *that* is poetry.
These are the only ways I know it.' – EMILY DICKINSON

'You only experience a thing when you can express it – however
haltingly – to your own mind.'– DOROTHY L. SAYERS

So, somehow you've managed to find some space in your head;
and, if you're lucky, you've found a place in the world – a corner
of the living-room table, a hut in the yard, a quiet room with book-
shelves and a desk – where you can read and write; you've found
time to be alone, when the others are out or asleep, time to talk to
yourself. Or you've time on your hands and a desire to give that
lonely conversation shape.

Whatever, you find space and time because you want to. An
appetite for words has become an addiction. Want becomes need
becomes will. If anything means work, this private indulgence does.
You are unique. Your brain and heart, your context and a particular sequence of events adds up to what you call your life, which is
a one-off. No one else has your raw material. There's a difference,
though, between experience and what happens to you. You have
to tell yourself what's happening in order to experience it. Is this
why you need space in your head? Space for your own words, the
exact words. If you habitually express yourself to yourself in stock
phrases, life itself becomes a cliché. If you choose your words, experience is enriched. Breaking the silence is as easy as breaking
wind, but it's hard work and huge pleasure distilling the babble,
translating the babel, between your own ears. 'Poetry is the music
of what happens' (Seamus Heaney).

Poetry is something both ordinary and extreme. It's talking, to
yourself and to others; it's doing it at a pitch of concentration and
focus; it's discovering a voice – perhaps not one, which may become
a monotone, but a repertoire of voices – or, better, your own idiom;
it's finding the language, with its sound in the air and its shape on

the page, that best reveals itself to the listening reader; it's finding your tongue. A poem provokes the response *Yes!* though the recognition may be of something strange. Housman said it stiffens the hair on the back of your neck. It strikes the solar plexus. It seems to add up to more than the sum of its words. As Auden said, it's a verbal contraption, *and* it's rooted in imaginative awe.

That, surely, is what seduced you: the rhymes and songs of childhood, readings and hymns, some helpings of the poetry purée dished up at school, lines from plays and films, fragments of radio, images landed live and thrashing from dreams, instants of contact with what Yeats called the Great Memory, moments when mere vocabulary expanded to fill a space in the spirit. Something in us looks back to a time of good talk, good crack by the fire, when ordinary words seemed to ignite – in a tale, a song, a verse, a poem – and became extraordinary. This is where, before paper and ink, the language of the tribe is purified, refined and driven forward wilfully to name objects and insights with new precision. A poet never forgets that this is where literature starts. In the dark, around a fire, comforted or blindingly discomfited by words.

So what did you meet when you went out to look for poetry? Dourly dressed slim volumes on the shelves with stiff blurbs appealing to an academic arrogance you didn't possess, doors to a club for which you didn't have the password. Anthologies with forewords like party political broadcasts preaching the latest poetical panacea. You wanted generosity and nourishment; you were offered a predominantly masculine world of sects and stances. Maybe you were lucky enough to come upon a shop that stocked on its rather dusty shelves the magazines and books that pour – the Muse be thanked – from the small presses. Here the manifestos could be even more preciously gnomic or extravagantly periphrastic, prefacing "experimental" lines that barely dislocated the banal or sentimental. Still, there was life on the shelves too. You found it or you wouldn't be reading this.

I had some tedious teachers. At fifteen, I failed my English Literature exam. I studied sciences at A level, though I had to carry on with English. It was different. Unconstrained by a syllabus, a teacher new to me enthused about the novels and poetry he loved. Suddenly I needed to write. Judiciously he praised and criticised my poems. I feasted on what W.H. Smith and my pocket afforded. I imitated T.S. Eliot, I blundered through Ezra Pound's *Cantos*. Then I discovered the stylish black covers of Penguin Modern Poets and found myself in the company of such as Elizabeth Jennings and R.S. Thomas, Peter Porter and Jack Clemo, Martin Bell and

8

Christopher Middleton, Allen Ginsberg and Lawrence Ferlinghetti. I worked in a laboratory for a year and by the time I went to read Botany and Philosophy at university I wanted to be a writer.

I attended English lectures when I should have been working. In a pub a black-bearded man, whose eyes were zealous for poetry, sold me a magazine. He gave me a glimpse of what life with words could be. He was Jon Silkin, the magazine was *Stand*. Then Penguin Modern European Poets began to appear. Summer in Greece was illuminated in retrospect by George Seferis and Odysseus Elytis. After graduation I went to Eastern Europe with Miroslav Holub, poet and scientist, in my pocket. I left Prague in August 1968, just before Soviet troops rolled in. The next year Tony Harrison edited an issue of *Stand* dedicated to new Czech writing.

These were rare moments when I felt in touch with real poetry in the real world. Mostly I felt isolated, hopelessly out of it. Then I'd discover Stevie Smith, an adamant imagination hiding beneath apparent whimsy, or Anna Akhmatova, whom Joseph Brodsky called 'the keening muse'. I visited my girlfriend in Manchester and found myself at a reading hosted by Harry Chambers (now Peterloo Poets): folk-singer David Hammond with poets Michael Longley and Seamus Heaney in a small room. They invited me to Belfast for the 1969 Festival. British troops had just arrived. Poetry was urgent, poets knew what they had to wrestle with.

A mixture of naive idealism and bloody-mindedness took me to a cottage outside London where I worked in lieu of rent and taught an evening class in order to eat. In order to be a poet. Well, I'd published apprentice pieces in university magazines, hadn't I? You can be hugely ambitious in a ghetto of the like-minded, or in a garret. I did some writing, learnt a bit about myself, got rejection slips. Then *Phoenix* took a poem, and the *New Statesman* took two. It's been up and down ever since.

That's a quick sketch of the way I got into poetry. Every writer's story is different. And similar. Most of us have no contacts, no inherited advantages, no keys to doors. However shaky or cocksure we are we have to write some poems we're happy to stand by. We dare to read them or show them to friends. We post them off to magazines. At every stage we risk being misunderstood, we risk rejection. That's the hardest thing, unless like a friend of mine you always say, and believe yourself when you say it, 'Fools, they're just not ready for me yet.'

You thought your poem was a poem was a poem. Then someone tells you it isn't a poem at all. Someone else praises it. You discover that poets, poetasters and poetry lovers are altogether human creatures, subject to frailty, to fads and factions. Sometimes, I tell you, it's hard to keep faith.

It's easier and very natural to huddle together for warmth with a group, a writers' circle that you can rely upon to pat you on the back, that reinforces and underwrites your notion of poetry. Better to find one that offers both support and tough criticism; you're fortunate if you do. On the other hand you may be, by choice or of necessity, a loner. Temperament may demand a little exile, a dark or ivory tower. Writing is a solitary – lone or lonely – business, by definition, but isolation can also be comfortable if you're insecure or arrogant enough, or both. Do you fear that poets of the past or your peers will influence you out of existence? Or were you cast in the role of the outsider? Some time, though, you should get your work out into the world and see your place in it. You want to write the poem that will change our perception of the twentieth or twenty-first century. You can hope. You should.

Getting into Poetry offers no recipe for literary stardom, no Stanislavsky method of poetic deportment. Nor does it tell you how to write poems, though it points in helpful directions. It is an orientation course for readers and writers of poetry who don't necessarily have English Literature degrees; it demystifies and illuminates the context in which we work, twentieth-century tradition and the current scene. It puts up signposts, which may point out destinations you want to reach, or whisper *Danger!* in your ear. It gives advice and information. It makes two rash assumptions about you: one, that you are arrogant or at least ambitious enough to be determined to find your way, to read and write well; two, that you are willing to look at yourself, the world of books, and the world which is your subject-matter and your audience with all the humility it takes.

CHAPTER TWO

A Sketch Map

'So fiercely our brains burn, we're driven to
Plunge down into the chasm, Hell or Heaven, who cares?
Deep down to the Unknown to find the new.'
— CHARLES BAUDELAIRE

'Literature is a place for generosity and affection and hunger
for equals – not a prize-fight ring...' – TILLIE OLSEN

I wouldn't even try to draw a detailed map of twentieth-century poetry in the small space I have here; but if you're a newcomer to the poetry scene, or feel that you're still a stranger, this chapter is a sketch map which aims to help you find your way about, to orientate yourself in the landscape you've chosen to inhabit. All maps are partial two-dimensional representations of reality, sketch maps especially so. I could decide that mountains are more useful landmarks than rivers, or that both are more significant than arbitrary boundary lines drawn to claim and disclaim territory with no reference to underlying geology.

I could choose a very few names who, in my opinion, sit fair and square in some poetic Great Tradition. I could argue that theirs, and theirs alone, are the voices that purify the language of the tribe. But I couldn't do it convincingly. For a start, I must use the plural: traditions, languages, tribes. I don't want to prospect for gold alone and spend my time refining and assaying it; I want to value the variety of precious metals and gems. While rejecting what's counterfeit or paste we can appreciate the richness of plurality; we can celebrate poetry's variousness.

Two women and a man

If you love poetry, you'll want to read back as far as you can, not looking nostalgically for some Golden Age – whether Anglo-Saxon, Afro-Caribbean, Celtic or whatever – but to discover the traditions that nourish you. This chapter's ambition is limited; it offers a foreshortened perspective in order to get to grips with the current context and to explain terms which you will come across when

11

reading about twentieth-century poetry. It sets up some finger-posts and some warning signs.

But first, a brief visit to the seventeenth century. Anne Bradstreet emigrated from Lincolnshire to the New World in 1630 when she was 18. She was white America's first poet. Her brother-in-law brought her work to London without her knowledge and it was published there in 1650 as *The Tenth Muse, Lately Sprung Up In America*. The poetry of hers now most valued was written later and published posthumously. Conrad Aiken set her firmly in the American canon; John Berryman addressed her in *Homage to Mistress Bradstreet*; Adrienne Rich identified with her. Bradstreet wrote:

> I am obnoxious to each carping tongue
> Who says my hand a needle better fits,
> A poet's pen all scorn I should thus wrong,
> For such despite they cast on female wits:
> If what I do prove well, it won't advance,
> They'll say it's stol'n, or else it was by chance.

Anne Bradstreet was a Puritan. Not so Aphra Behn, who was born in Kent and, on her return from a visit to Surinam in 1664, married a city merchant, Behn, who died soon afterwards. She lived by her wits, mostly as a playwright, novelist and poet. Virginia Woolf honours her as the first English woman to earn her living by writing. She turned the fashionable subject of the virgin seduced by the amorous shepherd on its head; her virgin's eagerness makes her seducer impotent – Maureen Duffy's biography of Behn is called *The Passionate Shepherdess* – and subsequently caused male anthologists to ignore her work. Her philosophical novel, *Oroonoko, or the History of the Royal Slave*, attacks the slave trade and white hypocrisy, while championing the character of black slaves and South American Indians.

George Moses Horton's poem, 'On Liberty and Slavery', is in many anthologies. In the first half of the nineteenth century his master hired him out as a servant to Chapel Hill University, North Carolina, for 50 cents a day. White students commissioned him to write them eloquent love poems, at 25 cents a time, whose passion and wit would impress their girlfriends and fiancées. This way he hoped to earn enough to buy his freedom; he didn't succeed, and remained a slave until the emancipation.

These poets make us think twice about literary history: the position of women writers in our culture; all that emigrants and colonists, the colonised and their independent heirs have given back to English; the legacy of the Middle Passage, Afro-Caribbean and Afro-American literature. It's not very long since women's writing,

Commonwealth writing and Black writing were regarded as side-shows at the literary circus.

Modernists to Martians

'…without Joyce, Eliot and Pound, the atmosphere of English literature today [early 1950s] would be that of the bar of a suburban golf club.' – EMRYS HUMPHREYS

Labels are stuck on poets and poetry, like anything else. The best labels are the titles of poems, titles on the spines of books, or the names of the poets themselves. It may be hard to say exactly what these labels name, but they're given: 'Kings' from *A Way of Looking* by Elizabeth Jennings. I could pin other labels on her – White, Woman, Oxford, Roman Catholic, etc – and I could add another, shared by several other poets: The Movement. She's a Movement poet because her work was published in the Movement anthology, *New Lines*, and because she reacted against the excesses of Modernism etc, etc. On the other hand it must be said that she doesn't share either the sardonic tone or the taste for irony that tend to characterise Movementeers…

So it goes. Critics, journalists, academics – and poets who are not above manifestos or name-calling – use labels to simplify and illuminate the world, then spend the rest of the daylight writing footnotes to qualify or side-step the terms they've invented. Poets change, to the chagrin of critics, and outgrow their labels too. Still, if you're trying to find your way around, a brief guide to the terms in common use is helpful.

Symbolists

Inspired by Baudelaire (1821-67), whom I quote at the head of this chapter, the poets Verlaine, Rimbaud, Mallarmé and others rejected naturalism and exchanged the attempt at an objective view of the world for deep subjectivism, characterised by the use of private, hermetic or occult symbols. They favoured suggestion rather than statement, evocation rather than description, mood rather than opinion. In their poetry they aimed for the purity of music, believing in sound's affinities with all the senses, and in correspondences between the senses and between spirit and matter. They gave us free verse (which they called *vers libre*) and the prose poem. Almost all the great Modernists were influenced by them. Their direct heirs were Rilke and Valéry, together with W.B. Yeats who brought

Symbolism into twentieth-century English; in the end, though, the masterful images deserted him; naked resolve was left:

> Now that my ladder's gone,
> I must lie down where all the ladders start,
> In the foul rag-and-bone-shop of the heart.

Modernists

Modernism is a portmanteau term for the experimental and avant-garde movements of the early twentieth century. Harold Rosenberg called it 'the tradition of the new'. Modernist writers turned against nineteenth-century conventions: traditional metre, realism, the consensus between author and reader. Verse could be free, and poets free of bourgeois values. Modernism's psyche was cosmopolitan, urban, stimulated by cultural variety and dislocation, fed from the Pandora's box of psychology and anthropology opened by Sigmund Freud and J.G. Frazer (*The Golden Bough*). Awareness of the unconscious, of the irrational, of relativism and alternative realities was reflected in techniques of juxtaposition, stream-of-consciousness, discontinuity and multiple point-of-view; collages of images, complex allusions and parodies contribute to the fragmentary nature of texts which challenge readers to discover their coherence. Critics have worried at the paradoxically reactionary nature of many modernists, and at the drift from all-too-human romanticism and naturalism towards dehumanisation. Modernism's landmarks include Ezra Pound's *Cantos*, which began to appear in 1917, the prose-poetry of James Joyce's *Ulysses* and T.S. Eliot's *The Waste Land*, both published in 1922, and Basil Bunting's *Briggflatts* (1966). Poets as diverse in character and intention as Hugh MacDiarmid and David Jones, whose influence has been seminal for Scottish and Welsh poetry, took what they needed from modernism. Some of its mannerisms and references are dated, but early modernist work often seems fresher than contemporary poetry. Pound's dictum was 'Make it new.' The best poets make it new and make it last. Anne Stevenson has said that Geoffrey Hill is perhaps the last of the great modernists.

Imagists

Imagism was a modernist movement (1912-17) which rebelled against Romanticism and "poetic" verbiage. Influenced by the Japanese tanka and haiku, it favoured the concise lyric founded on one image, free rhythms and musical cadence rather than regular metre, the precise image rather than symbolism or abstraction. Pound said, 'the natural object is always the adequate symbol.' He edited their first anthology, *Des Imagistes*, in 1914. Imagists included H.D. (Hilda

Doolittle), D.H. Lawrence, William Carlos Williams, F.S. Flint, Ford Madox Ford and Amy Lowell who, after Pound's defection to **Vorticism** (a movement, led by Wyndham Lewis, which celebrated the machine age) and the large-scale eclecticism of the *Cantos*, led the group and edited three more anthologies, *Some Imagist Poets* (1915-17). Pound coined 'Amy-gism'.

Georgians

Rupert Brooke, Edward Marsh (editor) and Harold Munro (publisher) planned a series of volumes, *Georgian Poetry*, of which five appeared (1912-22). Amongst the poets were W.H. Davies, John Masefield, Walter de la Mare, John Drinkwater and D.H. Lawrence; later volumes included Isaac Rosenberg, Edmund Blunden, Siegfried Sassoon and Robert Graves. The last three rejected the label Georgian; what Graves called their 'uncontroversial subjects' of rural and domestic life came to seem escapist when overtaken by the First World War. Though formally conservative, they were compelled to enlarge poetry's subject-matter. But Georgian became a perjorative term, and the enterprise was attacked by Pound, Eliot and the Sitwells. W.H. Auden wrote that the English landscape's 'gentleness can tempt those who love it into writing genteely'. Some critics have rewritten history to exclude good poets from the Georgians and include only the mediocre. But half the poets represented in the anthologies are now highly regarded and the term Georgian is sometimes stretched to include Edward Thomas and other non-modernist poets of the period.

War Poets

The poets of the First World War did not belong to one movement, they were claimed by the same cataclysm. They should be read in, for example, *The Penguin Book of First World War Poetry* (ed. Jon Silkin). I won't write about them here, except to say that many of them brought a Georgian sensibility to the trenches and forged poetry out of its collision with the pity and pitilessness of war using the equipment they had to hand. Modernist temperaments should, in theory, have been more suited to the task, but their war poems came later.

Surrealists

Ushered in by Dada (French word for 'hobby-horse', plucked at random from the dictionary), a movement founded in Zurich and New York in 1916: an anarchic protest against a culture discredited by the First World War; its nihilistic manifestos denied all sense of order. Surrealism's first manifesto, by André Breton, was published in Paris in 1924. It explored the boundaries of the rational and irrational, the conscious and unconscious, dreams and waking, hallucination and reality, sanity and madness, drawing on Symbolism and Freud, and later trying to reconcile Freud with Marx. Its poets – Breton, Aragon, Desnos, Éluard, etc – experimented with automatic writing to achieve the spontaneous coupling of unrelated objects, the surreal poetic image. David Gascoyne published *A Short Survey of Surrealism* in 1935 and, following the International Surrealist Exhibition of 1936, an English group, that included Gascoyne and Herbert Read, was founded. In the same year Gascoyne's *Man's Life is His Meat* was published, followed by *Hölderlin's Madness* in 1938. He suffered from the Surrealist label, for critics failed to understand the scale and painful conscientiousness of his later development. Surrealism's influence shows in the work of Dylan Thomas, George Barker, Roy Fisher, Christopher Middleton, Jeremy Reed.

Cambridge Critics

A school of criticism which redrew the poetic map in the 1920s and 30s. I.A. Richards, with F.R. and Q.D. Leavis and the poet William Empson, rejected biographical and historical ways of approaching poets and poetry in favour of close reading of texts, **Practical Criticism**. (Empson later attacked neglect of biography in criticism.) Influenced by S.T. Coleridge and by Eliot, whose notion of the dissociation of sensibility suggested the divorce of thought and feeling in poetry since John Donne, they looked for reintegration of head and heart, for moral seriousness and life-enhancement, and for subtlety and complexity (Empson's *Seven Types of Ambiguity*) in poems. The Cambridge School created the atmosphere for the poets of the Movement. F.R. Leavis's teaching and his magazine *Scrutiny* had a profound influence on the teaching of English Literature in Britain in the post-war period.

Pylon Poets

Stephen Spender's poem 'The Pylons' provided the nickname for the group of young left-wing poets of the 1930s that included W.H. Auden, C. Day Lewis and Louis MacNeice; imagery drawn from the contemporary industrial landscape was a calculated component of their work. They shared both a radical posture in the face of public chaos, and a conservative approach to technique, following Hardy rather than Eliot, though they experimented fluently with traditional forms in poetry which might be lyrical, pastoral, urbane, public or personal – all of those in Auden's case.

16

The New Apocalypse

A group of anti-cerebral writers who venerated D.H. Lawrence and espoused stormy and surreal imagery to encompass their 'large, accepting attitude to life': a romantic rejection of Auden's intellectual classicism. They included J.F. Hendry, Henry Treece and G.S. Fraser; their anthologies spanned the Second World War: *The New Apocalypse* (1940), *The White Horseman* (1941) and *The Crown and the Sickle* (1945). Poets more or less associated with the group included Dylan Thomas, Vernon Watkins, George Barker, W.S. Graham and David Gascoyne.

Other Names

Many important poets aren't associated with groups and, as you'd expect, don't line up neatly in critical formation. A portrait of groups and movements is a caricature of a period's poetic life. Some cautionary examples: Edwin Muir, Patrick Kavanagh, Austin Clarke, Stevie Smith, Robert Graves, John Betjeman, Elizabeth Daryush, Charles Causley, Alun Lewis, Keith Douglas, Kathleen Raine...

The Movement

The name was coined by J.D. Scott (*The Spectator*, 1954) for a group of writers including Philip Larkin, Kingsley Amis, Donald Davie, D.J. Enright, Robert Conquest, John Wain, Elizabeth Jennings and Thom Gunn. The Movement's ethos was sceptical, robust, ironic, anti-romantic and anti-Apocalyptic; two anthologies define it: *Poets of the 1950s* (ed. Enright, 1955) and *New Lines* (ed. Conquest, 1956). Conquest wrote of 'a negative determination to avoid bad principles', and for Larkin and Amis these included modernism and internationalism; while Davie and Gunn were drawn towards America by different routes, and Jennings' work outgrew the Movement's rational contraints. By 1957 its members were disowning it; Wain declared, 'Its work is done.'

The Group

Founded in Cambridge in 1952, the Group continued under Philip Hobsbaum's chairmanship in London from 1955. It was a workshop, rather than a movement, in which poetry or prose was read aloud by the author and critically discussed. Among its participants were Peter Redgrove, Peter Porter, Alan Brownjohn, Edward Lucie-Smith, George MacBeth, Martin Bell and, after Lucie-Smith became chairman in 1959, Fleur Adcock and B.S. Johnson. From Bell's poem 'Mr Hobsbaum's Monday Evening Meeting': 'Below the ceiling, guardian of the Grail/The ghost of Dr Leavis floats...'

A Group Anthology (ed. Hobsbaum and Lucie-Smith) was published in 1963. Hobsbaum later moved to Belfast (see **Ireland**, below).

The New Poetry

Not a group but an influential anthology selected by Al Alvarez, published by Penguin in 1962 (revised 1966). It includes Movement and Group poets, but its introduction's subtitle is 'Beyond the Gentility Principle'. Alvarez asks what happened to the innovations of Pound and Eliot, why is 1950s poetry so narrow, academic, polite in the face of cultural disintegration, world wars, genocide, nuclear threat. His selection opens with four Americans: John Berryman, Robert Lowell, Anne Sexton, Sylvia Plath; it represents British poets not on the London/Oxbridge axis: Norman MacCaig, R.S. Thomas, Iain Crichton Smith, and poets alert to modernism, to Europe and America: Michael Hamburger, Christopher Middleton, Charles Tomlinson; it concludes with poets born in the 1930s such as Ted Walker, Jon Silkin and Ted Hughes. Some at least of the contributors seemed immune to gentility and exhibited the naked seriousness, openness and integrity which Alvarez argued should ideally be allied with skill and formal intelligence.

American Voices

Look back to Walt Whitman and compare the large unconscious scenery of the mind in 'President Lincoln's Funeral Hymn' with the claustrophobia of his contemporary Tennyson's 'In Memoriam'. See Pound breaking the pentameter and juxtaposing images, scenes and episodes on an epic scale. Admire the imagination triumphant in the making of Wallace Stevens' supreme fictions; 'Piece the world together, boys, but not with your hands.' Understand William Carlos Williams' urgent need to make a truly American tune, a new measure, out of 'the words we need to get back to, words washed clean'. Charles Olson prescribed a **Projective Verse** in which traditional forms, syntax, punctuation, description and simile should not impede the flow of energy, the progress from perception to perception, should allow the poem to breathe as the poet breathes, allow the ear to hear the syllable (a secret lost between the late Elizabethans and Pound), without permitting the poet's ego to stifle content/form; this verse is **Open Form** rather than closed. Olson and his followers – Robert Creeley, Robert Duncan, Denise Levertov, Ed Dorn, Jonathan Williams, etc – are called **Black Mountain Poets** because they were associated with Black Mountain College or *Black Mountain Review*.

Duncan was also – with Helen Adam, Lawrence Ferlinghetti,

Jack Spicer, etc – part of the **San Francisco Renaissance**, while *Black Mountain Review* also published Allen Ginsberg and Gregory Corso who, with Jack Kerouac, Gary Snyder, William Burroughs and others, came to be known as the **Beat Generation**. For them drugs, wheels, sex and Zen Buddhism were means towards ecstasy and enlightenment, and away from conventional, puritanical *mores*. They looked back to Blake, Shelley, Whitman, Rimbaud and the Black Mountain; they had a powerful influence on 1960s counter-culture: Voznesensky and Yevtushenko, Bob Dylan and the Beatles.

The work of the **New York Poets** (including Barbara Guest, Kenneth Koch, Frank O'Hara, James Schuyler and John Ashbery) is intimate with the art world and able to incorporate high art and popular culture – flippantly or subversively abolishing the distinc-tion – into multi-voiced, all-embracing or all-dismantling visions of the world: characteristics that belong to **Postmodernism**. These voices (the Black Mountain, Beats, New York Poets, etc) were brought together in an anthology which was seminal for many poets on this side of the Atlantic: *The New American Poetry 1945-1960* (ed. Donald M. Allen) whose revised edition was subtitled *The Postmoderns*.

Alvarez's Americans, in contrast, were **Confessional Poets** who worked in a very naked mode. Theodore Roethke's personal poems and Allen Ginsberg's *Howl* (1956), an apocalyptic elegy for the American Dream, made possible candid autobiographical accounts of previously unmentionable distress. Robert Lowell dealt with divorce and mental breakdowns, Anne Sexton with abortion and with life in mental hospitals, John Berryman with alcoholism and insanity, Sylvia Plath with suicide and W.D. Snodgrass with divorce. Their undeniable power and the suicides of Berryman, Sexton and Plath fostered the identification of inner torment with poetic brilliance.

Peter Forbes has said that 'the last great Anglo-American was Robert Lowell', though poets like Galway Kinnell, Charles Simic, Louis Simpson, Anthony Hecht, Adrienne Rich, C.K. Williams, Stephen Dobyns, Dave Smith, Sharon Olds, Dana Gioia and Amy Clampitt have fans and followers over here. Because poets from this side of the Atlantic – like Seamus Heaney, Paul Muldoon, and James Lasdun – can make a living in America, whereas our universities are not as welcoming, current American poetry seeps rather than flows in this direction. Contrasting trends include the natural and sincere, the **New Formalism**, and **Language Poets** (the 1980s magazine L=A=N=G=U=A=G=E) who focus upon the 'non-referential use of language': Rimbaud talked of the poet becoming visionary 'by a long, drastic and deliberate disordering of the senses'; for 'senses' Language Poets read 'sentences'.

Links
Vachel Lindsay's 'The Congo' (1914) and Langston Hughes' work with musicians in the late 1930s led on to Jazz Poetry of the 1950s with Kenneth Patchen, Kenneth Rexroth and Amiri Baraka (Le Roi Jones) which, together with the Beats, inspired British poets as various as Christopher Logue, William Scammell, Roy Fisher, Michael Horovitz, Pete Brown, Spike Hawkins and Libby Houston. The work of these demonstrates the variety of ways in which influences are absorbed. There are no simple genealogies. Just as American poets often responded to European predecessors as rather than British/Irish ones, so the latter also looked to French or German, Eastern European or Scandinavian examples.

Underground Poets
Between the late 1950s and mid-1970s, anti-hierarchical, anti-war (Vietnam, the Bomb) protest poetry drew, superficially or more deeply, on the explosion of possibilities, on the range of open form, experimental work and on the folk-song tradition. Writers like Adrian Mitchell, Jeff Nuttall, Tom Pickard, Alexander Trocchi, Heathcote Williams and the Liverpool Poets thumbed their noses at the London literary scene, performed their work at readings and events, and published in little magazines. Nuttall portrays the aspirations of an alternative society living in the nuclear shadow, his experience of the post-war avant-garde, in *Bomb Culture*. Michael Horovitz anthologised its work in *Children of Albion: Poetry of the 'Underground' in Britain* (1969) and in his sequel *Grandchildren of Albion: Voices and Visions of Younger Poets in Britain* (1992) which chiefly documents the work of 1980s rock lyricists, alternative cabaret writers and performance poets.

Concrete Poets
What used to be known as **Pattern Poetry**, in which words are arranged on the page to picture a thing or a movement which corresponds with the poem's content, has roots at least as early as fourth-century BC Greece. George Herbert's 'Easter Wings' is an example. In Guillaume Apollinaire's 'Il pleut' words trickle down the page. Influenced by Dada and Hans Arp, the Concrete Poetry movement was launched in São Paulo in 1956. Much of it dispenses with linearity and, using space as a structural agent, aims to be perceived whole, relieved of the burden of 'ideas, symbolic ref-

20

erence, allusion and repetitious emotional content'. Bob Cobbing and Peter Finch are practitioners, and the Scottish input is important: Ian Hamilton Finlay's works approach the condition of sculpture, while Edwin Morgan's are more verbal.

Modernists, Postmodernists and Post-postmodernists

Where and when the movements begin and end is a matter of dispute and of supreme indifference to many writers. I have attempted a definition of modernism above; as I have hinted, postmodernism is a culture of fragmentary images and styles, flickering and evanescent as in TV, advertising and videos, high art and pop mingled. Postmodernism is often characterised as the selective intensification of certain modernist techniques and effects. The modernist poet struggled with dislocated and disintegrating material to achieve coherence through formality, myth and symbol; the postmodernist delights in the confusion and may playfully assemble deliberately depthless works from it.

While big publishers mostly turned their backs on modernism and its children, things happened elsewhere. Tom Raworth's *Big Green Day*. Basil Bunting's *Briggflatts*. His followers Barry Mac-Sweeney and Tom Pickard in Newcastle. Allen Fisher's **Place** project in South London. J.H. Prynne's *The White Stones*, and his **Cambridge School** which includes Andrew Crozier, Peter Riley, Wendy Mulford, John James and John Riley. Adrian Henri, Brian Patten, Henry Graham and Roger McGough in Liverpool. Roy Fisher's *A Furnace* and Gael Turnbull in Birmingham. Lee Harwood in Brighton and, more recently, Peter Didsbury in Hull. And so on. The imprints most strongly identified with postmodernist poetry in Britain in the 1960s were Fulcrum Press and *Grosseteste Review*; then as now the small presses were its most active propagators, but just recently John Muckle and Iain Sinclair have given some of these postmodern poets their first commercial publishing outlet through their editorship of the short-lived Paladin poetry list.

Languages and Tribes

At the start of this chapter I said that we must use the plural: traditions, languages, tribes. All poets must create their own idiom, and from a variety of linguistic starting points. In only a fraction of Britain and Ireland is Standard English the first language. This is a source of richness.

It is also the root of doubt, of psychic ambiguity, of the search for identity. It can lead to the ghetto, to a necessary nationalism and ethnic pride defined in opposition to the white male power-base, a London seen as incorrigibly provincial. It can lead through retrenchment and embattled exclusivity to the celebration of plurality, to internationalism and possibly (not probably) to a poetic republic where dialect and patois, gender and blood (I mean Welsh, Jamaican etc) are neither advantages nor impediments. Some hope. But a hope that should undergird the struggle.

It is commonly held as axiomatic that the most successful poets are Oxbridge-educated, work in academia or publishing and live within reach of London; equally, that the finest poets are outsiders who live and work a long way from London.

Scotland

Iain Crichton Smith has expressed the pain of being torn between two tongues, Gaelic and English, and the problem of commitment to one or the other. He writes in both, as do a number of younger poets. Sorley Maclean's Gaelic output reaches English-speakers in translation. Robert Garioch collaborated with Maclean in Scots and English. Hugh MacDiarmid – nationalist, internationalist and catalyst of the Scottish Renaissance – wrote, like Burns, in synthetic Scots as well as English. Norman MacCaig, George Mackay Brown, G.F. Dutton, Stewart Conn and Alan Bold, and many younger poets such as Andrew Greig and Kathleen Jamie work in English. Some plumb the rural oral tradition of the North-East. Tom Leonard exploits the vigorous Glaswegian patois. W.N. Herbert has inherited and created his own Scots vernacular. The Lallans (lowland Scots) of Sydney Goodsir Smith and Alexander Scott can draw less and less upon a spoken tongue. However, Robert Crawford has attacked Edwin Muir's notion that Scottish literature has been disabled by a confusion of tongues and needs a homogeneous language if it is to achieve autonomy; Crawford sees purity of language as a dead end and argues that Scots poetry is richer for its promiscuous verbal cocktail: Lallans, English, the gutter and the dictionary, fed also by European and American influences, and by translations such as those of Edwin Morgan (Mayakovsky's *Wi the Haill Voice*), Robert Garioch (the poems of Belli and Apollinaire) and Liz Lochhead (Molière's *Tartuffe*). Viva polyphony!

Ireland

Tom Paulin remembers the discomfort, when studying English at Hull, of transcribing Ulster sounds into Received Pronunciation. Seamus Heaney says, 'Our guttural muse / was bulled long ago / by the alliterative tradition...' and, in 'Broagh', relishes 'that last / *gh* the strangers found / difficult to manage'. Paul Muldoon's first published poems were written in Irish, abandoned later for lack of real control of the language. In 'To Derek Mahon' Michael Longley writes of the politics of language before the Troubles, the undertow, 'Moonlight glossing the confusions / Of its each bilingual wave'. John Montague, John Hewitt and Philip Hobsbaum fuelled the Northern Renaissance. Hobsbaum began the Belfast Group in the sixties; Stewart Parker (the playwright), James Simmons, Longley, Heaney and others were transformed by it, as Heaney has written, from craven provincials into genuine parochials. The ethos for Michael Longley and Derek Mahon's generation was post-Movement, neo-Georgian; they found their own routes back to Patrick Kavanagh, Louis MacNeice or W.B. Yeats. The Ulster poets found ways to artfully confront or evade the political situation with hints and half-stories, with inner exile and 'Whatever you say, say nothing.' In Ireland at large there hasn't been an identifiable literary movement since Yeats' time, though trends elsewhere have had their effect; Brendan Kennelly has taken on the nightmare of history and made it and the present shockingly contemporaneous in large-scale works such as *Cromwell* and *The Book of Judas*; other Dublin poets, notably Dermot Bolger and Michael O'Loughlin, whose patron is Anthony Cronin, have striven to create an urban realist poetry in reaction against ruralism.

This tension and the relationship between Irish and English language poetry are variously refracted in the work of Thomas Kinsella, Paul Muldoon, Eiléan Ní Chuilleanáin, Eavan Boland, Medbh McGuckian, Nuala Ní Dhomhnaill, Paul Durcan, Gerald Dawe, Ciaran Carson, Bernard O'Donoghue, John Ennis, Dennis O'Driscoll and many more; the scene, and the search for Irish identity, is lively, punctuated by critical outbursts and pained silences. Political divisions in literature are polarised in the continuing critical debate between Derry's Field Day, with its nationalist programme of theatre and publishing (backed by a committee of writers including Seamus Heaney, Seamus Deane, Tom Paulin, David Hammond and, until recently, Brian Friel), and the "revisionist" opposition headed by the formidable Belfast critic Edna Longley.

Wales
'I play on a small pipe, a little aside from the main road. But thank you for listening.' So said R.S. Thomas with his tongue in his cheek. Or his tongues. The Anglo-Welsh tradition was first mapped by A.G. Prys-Jones' anthology *Welsh Poets* (1917). Welsh writers are too little known outside Wales, apart from those living in England like Dannie Abse and Leslie Norris, and of course the Thomases:

Dylan's passionate metaphysical rhetoric and R.S.'s bleak pastoral tempered by hard-won spiritual comfort, seen, despite their breadth, as twin facets of a national caricature. Parochialism on both sides of Offa's Dyke has a lot to answer for. Some ardent poets are incomers like Raymond Garlick, Jean Earle and Nigel Wells. Others respond vigorously to European influences in the tradition of Vernon Watkins. There is a divide, crudely North-South in the mind, between those who look back to Dafydd ap Gwilym and the forms of Welsh poetry, to techniques such as *cynghanedd* (internal rhyme and repetition of consonants as assimilated into English by Gerard Manley Hopkins), and those who don't, however hotly they engage with Welsh issues. Hear Roland Mathias's dense and dexterous landscapes, vivid and grieving, John Tripp's political and confessional vehemence, Gillian Clarke's celebrations, distinctive and archetypical, and Tony Conran's re-working of a 6th century lament in his elegy for the Welsh dead of the Falklands War. There are those who escape like Oliver Reynolds, and those who root themselves triumphantly: Sheenagh Pugh, Tony Curtis, Christine Evans, Robert Minhinnick and Hilary Llewellyn-Williams. They should be heard more widely. And there was David Jones, the great modernist who, despite his engagement with the *Mabinogion*, the matter of Wales and of Britain, is not often part of the chatter at the bardic breakfast table. Perhaps that's because he lived in Wales for such a short time.

Black Poets

In 'Island Muse' John Lyons sings, 'I come with my pen / from cool green forest'; John Agard, in 'Listen Mr Oxford Don', says 'mugging de Queen's English / is the story of my life'. The poet writes in white on black, as Gordon Rohlehr has argued in a discussion of Kamau Brathwaite's work; the imposed language was white, the ground of being is black. Otherwise, as Fred D'Aguiar has said, two black poets have no more in common than any two poets pulled out of a hat. They are multi-national and often multilingual in ways that transcend the old debate about Standard-English/Nation-Language and literary/oral traditions. There are shared histories: D'Aguiar's *Mama Dot* embodies the reality of slavery, colonialism, exploitation and independence; Derek Walcott, who is a major influence on poets this side of the Atlantic, has given these subjects homeric gravitas in *Omeros*. Grace Nichols' *I is a long-memoried woman* sprang from a dream she had about a young African girl, garlanded with flowers, swimming from Africa to the Caribbean, cleansing the ocean of ancestral suffering. Faustin Charles speaks of 'the survivor imagining home'; Jean Binta Breeze's mad woman raves, 'Mi waan go a country go look mango'; David Dabydeen writes of marking his mother's memory with songs and 'Poems that scrape bowl and bone / In English basements far from home'. First inspired by the poetry of the Old Testament, Linton Kwesi Johnson discovered that music entered poetry when he began to write in the Jamaican language; Reggae poetry, Dub poetry (his terms), Rhythm poetry and Rapso – performed, recorded and published – clearly confront British racism, police brutality, corrupt Babylon, and celebrate sex, music, ganja, the dream of Zion and other Rastafarian themes. The work of Michael Smith, Valerie Bloom, Benjamin Zephaniah, Lemn Sissay and others has reached a wide audience. James Berry is supremely conscious of the black poet's reverse missionary-role for British natives. In sensuous anguished poetry that draws on Seferis and Baudelaire as much as Creole, A.L. Hendriks explores the black diaspora, and the dislocation implicit in the mulatto, and the human condition. For Jackie Kay celebration and pain are rooted in a Glasgow childhood. Two languages maybe – Standard-English and Nation-Language that Brathwaite released from the dungeon of dialect – but many voices that need not be limited or ghettoised either by white prejudice or by self-censorship. E.A. Markham writes as Markham, but has also used the pseudonyms Paul St Vincent, a young black inner-city survivor, and Sally Goodman, a non-black feminist.

Women Poets

More than half of us are women. That's a big tribe, and one whose writers have needed to take control of man-made language, take power in publishing and be heard. When I first read poetry it was easy to assume that only a few exceptional women wrote it. Fleur Adcock recalls that the poets she read were male, and Denise Levertov that her favourites were all men. Publishers and anthologists made sure of it, and in selecting from the poems of, say, Elizabeth Barrett Browning, Charlotte Mew or Patricia Beer, chose what did not disturb the accepted notion of what women should write about. In 'Anger lay by me all night long' Elizabeth Daryush says, 'He... Struck from my hand the book, the pen...' The accepted notion has been passionately rejected and the last twenty years have seen a flowering of women's poetry in print, to the point where Carol Rumens wrote of feminism as both a springboard and an obstacle, and described the contents of her Chatto anthology *Making for the Open* as 'Post-Feminist Poetry'. Introducing her section of *The New British Poetry*, Gillian Allnutt called it 'Quote Feminist Unquote

Poetry' because to put any such tag in front of poetry is to constrain it. We look back to women who enlarged it, to Emily Dickinson, Anna Akhmatova, and Marina Tsvetayeva who was for her translator, Elaine Feinstein, a teacher of courage; Stevie Smith wrote of Poetry, 'She is an Angel, very strong...and never has any kindness at all...All the poet has to do is listen.' And where else than in Sylvia Plath, asks Allnutt, 'can you find such a threatening, cold, alien moon?' Anne Sexton and Denise Levertov have written toughly of love and pain and politics, and Adrienne Rich mapped out 'the new psychic geography'. Women have always been charged with lack of range, in subject and emotion, with lack of humour, with embroidery of the trivial and domestic, with spiritual posturing, with lamenting their lot. Well-known male poets can be slotted into the dock on all counts, and the charges are laughable in the light of the work of, for example, Sylvia Kantaris, Alison Fell, Fleur Adcock, Elizabeth Bartlett, Michèle Roberts, Nicki Jackowska, Frances Horovitz, Helen Dunmore, Jo Shapcott, Carol Ann Duffy and many others. Women are both charged with subjectivity and excluded from the male notion of 'I': ego mastering id, with female ego as male id's mistress; we all live with, and must heal these lesions. Women became authors of their own lives just as postmodernism deconstructed the whole idea, and schizophrenically disrupted the psyche while radical female connections were being forged, and correspondences recognised. Jeni Couzyn writes, 'The message of men is linear...the message of women is love...' Dr Animus and his wife Anima, in Anne Stevenson's 'Small Philosophical Poem', are not to be explained so easily. She has said that 'no artist can be optimistic in days of spiritual decay, but it is possible to be honest. And joyful.' Levertov writes, 'this day I see // the world, a word / intricately incarnate...'

Martians and other Earthlings

James Fenton coined the term 'the Martian School' to describe the work of Craig Raine and Christopher Reid; Raine's second book, *A Martian Sends a Postcard Home*, and Reid's first, *Arcadia*, were both published in 1979. They were also called the Metaphor Men, the New Elizabethans and the New Fantasticals, but Martian stuck. They and others like them – Michael Hofmann, Matthew Sweeney, Oliver Reynolds etc – were notable for the surprising visual metaphors they employed, for extended similes or conceits which had critics comparing them with the Metaphysical poets; the domestic, the everyday were playfully defamiliarised. They made the familiar strange; their detractors berated them for mere cleverness, for reinventing banal emotions and tired thoughts in gaudy tongues, for making the ludic use of words (language-play) a substitute for grappling with strong feelings and challenging ideas; their admirers claimed that because their poems obliged us to see freshly and sensuously, we had to think and feel again.

The ludic seems to make works postmodern that may otherwise be reactionary in form and content. The Narrative School, led by Andrew Motion, borrowed from the novel what postmodern novelists had abandoned. The labels are quickly chucked in the bin by practitioners if not by commentators. We find that Norman MacCaig had been living on Mars for years, that poets never stop telling stories. We move on to New Formalists like Lawrence Sail, Philip Gross, Elizabeth Garrett and James Lasdun, or to New Lyricism and New Colloquialism. The lines on the map are very shaky because we are too close to the ground. The monologue was suddenly and rightly valued in the work of Carol Ann Duffy and U.A. Fanthorpe, though poets had been doing it in different voices for ages. Duffy also qualified for the 80s Tough School with the likes of Sean O'Brien, Ken Smith and Tony Harrison. The last two have long developed contrasting idioms which embrace the personal and the political in breadth and depth; it is usually fruitless to categorise fine poets. Perhaps we should just read rather than pigeon-hole Jeffrey Wainwright, Rodney Pybus and Matt Simpson.

Is it worth penning the Light Verse hard man John Whitworth in one corral with Gavin Ewart and Kit Wright? Better to read them and judge. Is a woman poet, such as Wendy Cope or Fiona Pitt-Kethley, more likely to make the trendy set if her muse is comic or priapic? What of the Hull Group nurtured by Douglas Dunn? Sean O'Brien, Peter Didsbury, Douglas Houston and others are in no way provincial; all make their own treaties with the past and speak in surprising *fin-de-siècle* voices. Simon Armitage and Ian Duhig, amongst others, have been labelled Punk Modernists, for their combination of street-cred language, bizarre humour and learning. And how shall we classify Glyn Maxwell, Jackie Kay, Gerald Dawe, Robert Crawford, Maura Dooley and Martyn Crucefix? Align them if you like, but hope they'll outgrow your categories. Stitch up a hold-all, like New Generation Poets, and hope you can sell all the books it contains. It's good to be sceptical about hypes and groups and tags and movements: this chapter demonstrates that it's quite possible to sketch their story and leave out, or barely mention, many big names. Chapter 14 will, I hope, make up for that.

27

Hype

So poetry, which is in Oxford made
An art, in London only is a trade.
— JOHN DRYDEN

Beware of hype. Since poetry stopped being drably presented, content with its élitist minority appeal, the race has been on to sell it hard, to pit one contender against another, to promote a select group in the marketplace while ignoring the majority. Oxford University Press until recently claimed 'one of the finest lists of contemporary poetry'; now its advertisements trumpet unashamedly, 'The World's Finest Poetry'. Faber & Faber proclaim 'The Great Tradition Continues', implicitly linking their current list with Pound, Auden and Eliot; the great Faber helicopter tour (actually a couple of hops) by Raine and Heaney has entered the mythology of poetry marketing. Bloodaxe claim to publish 'Poetry with an Edge' which is 'a cut above the rest', implying both literary quality and contemporary relevance; editor Neil Astley describes the Bloodaxe approach as 'combining mischief with effrontery, suggesting a radical line, a pointed sense of humour, and a poetry list which is varied, lively and authoritative...now is that hype, marketing or literary analysis?'

Anthology hype: the trick here is to convince people – especially libarians and those who write school syllabuses – that your anthology is definitive and representative. *The Penguin Book of Contemporary British Poetry*'s introduction claims that it offers what 'a number of close observers' think of as the new British poetry. Close observers of the Martian and Narrative kind. Twenty white poets, six of them Irish, five women. However much critics admired the poets it was hard to see how the work, as brought together here, was a departure 'exhibiting something of the spirit of postmodernism', or a brilliant landmark, the first major anthology since Alvarez's *The New Poetry*.

Paladin's *The New British Poetry* claimed to represent what had not been acknowledged in the 'self-elected "mainstream" ' – to be 'wide-ranging', 'unique and ground-breaking' and 'accessible'. Eighty-five poets in four parts: a good black section, a good women's section, plus open form poets of the 1960s and 70s (hardly new), and younger postmodernist poets (some of whom are hardly accessible). New British Poetry, perhaps. But *The*? All anthologies are and must be partial. The trick for the reader is to study a number of them and not be taken in by inflated blurbs.

Discovered Genius hype: Sue Lenier's work was vigorously promoted in 1982. Donald Davie's opinion that her book should never have been published, and Christopher Reid's strictures on her antiquated style and lack of originality were quoted in order to show how mistaken anyone was who did not know her to be the best poet since Shakespeare. Academics knew: John Newton said that English poetry had been transformed overnight; W.W. Robson was convinced she was better than Ted Hughes; John Rathmell saw in her 'a much bigger thing' than Sylvia Plath. Enough said.

Undiscovered Genius hype: Bryan Appleyard celebrated the posthumous publication of his friend Kevin Stratford's poems (Carcanet Press, 1991) by comparing his qualities with those of Auden, Eliot and Ashbery. Fair enough. But his fury that Faber, Chatto and all mainstream publishers and literary magazines neglected Stratford led him to write off all that they have published in the last forty years, and to set the poetry of 'the most talented writer of my generation' against Heaney and Hughes's 'sad, contrived narrowness' and Larkin's 'small-minded depravity'.

I too feel passionate about poetry that I believe in, but I want to celebrate poetry's variousness. We must use the plural: traditions, languages, tribes. Landmarks in this sketch map of modern poetry are pointed out in Chapter 14, which is a reader's guide. There you'll find a selective listing of important poetry collections, influential anthologies and significant individual poems. If you're new to the landscape, some of the signposts and warnings in this chapter will be useful to you. But don't rely on them; read widely for yourself, with an open mind and a generous heart. Be critical, but not until you've earned the right. Feed your imagination, not your prejudices, and discover what nourishes and enlarges your taste. And don't believe all the labels. Draw your own map.

CHAPTER THREE

Waterholes

'I never read books – I write them.' – PUNCH, 1878

'People who say they love poetry and never buy any are a bunch of cheap sons-of-bitches.' – KENNETH PATCHEN

'I have my own voice. I meditate here, at this particular point, my psyche where time and eternity intersect, and I tune in. I get it straight from the source. So much clever writing by those who call themselves poets is like static on the air-waves, interference. It puts me off, knocks me off balance. I have to be centred, receptive, alive to my own unconscious. I keep myself unsullied, a pure channel for the Muse. I'd like you to read this. Set aside some time. Tell me what you feel. Tell me if you think everyone should read it.'

'I don't give a toss for all that literary crap. What does that stuff mean on the street, man? That's an élitist wank, that culture with a capital C. For the establishment, for the fat professors who lick the politicians' arses. I speak it like it is, I write it down so kids on the street can hear it, so it's relevant. You can stuff your big buildings full of books. Who's listening? They're listening to me. They would be, if some bastard would publish me. You want to read my stuff? You better, you might learn something.'

'I don't read much poetry, especially not modern stuff. Haven't got time. Bad enough finding the time to write my own. Anyway, modern poets don't seem to know what real poetry is. They haven't got the patience to rhyme properly. Poetry is my way of celebrating things. If there's a birth or a death or an anniversary in the family I write a poem. If there's a famine or a war, a rape or a pollution incident on the News that really moves me, although I'm so busy I find some time to put it down on paper. I wish modern poets wrote to move people. If people read my collection they'd see what I mean, they'd see the difference. You take it. I'd love to know your reaction. Careful, this carrier bag's not very strong.'

And so on...so many voices, more banal and more extreme, all implying that the previous two chapters are irrelevant. Cynical, perhaps, to parody them, but I'm dismayed by the number of would-be poets who almost boast that they don't read, even though they are motivated enough to come on a writing course. They love it though, oh yes, they love poetry.

There are periods when, immersed in your own work, it's wise not to read. There are poets whom I've had to avoid for a while because their influence so surreptitiously insinuates itself. Then I grow through that phase and the danger is past. They are dangerous because they are powerful; I'd rather risk the danger than miss the poetry. A poet of any age who's afraid of reading poetry, or petulantly dismissive of it, is going through aesthetic adolescence; doesn't want to see him or herself in an adult context; is fearful of not measuring up. All I can say is, grow up, wise up. Read, read, read. Discriminate. Make choices based on experience of books. Subscribe to magazines, use libraries, haunt bookshops. Quench your thirst fearlessly. Irrigate the imagination. Why wander in a desert wilfully avoiding the oases, filtering your own urine because it tastes so, so good?

Libraries

There are waterholes. If all the people who wrote poetry borrowed poetry books from public libraries, the shelves would be a lot richer. Libraries are under threat. They are having to decide, for instance, not to buy any novels this year, or to cut back on specialist or minority-interest titles. Use your local library; ask for the books you want and, if they won't buy them for your branch, for a few pence the LASER inter-library loan service will obtain them from elsewhere, from a public or university library at the other end of the country if need be. I used to order books from the mobile library that stopped once a fortnight in the hamlet where I lived. One was rare and difficult to get. But it came almost to my door, and when I'd finished with it I returned it to the branch library in town because I happened to be going there. The woman at the desk looked warily at the spine. 'I don't think it's one of ours, me dear.' She opened it and saw The British Library label. 'Oooh,' she said, 'I see,' and I swear she gave a kind of curtsey and did whatever librarians do when they're crossing themselves.

I'm saying that it's a wonderful service. It's under threat. Use it to the full. Cajole librarians. Encourage them in hard times. Insist they get the books you want. Support them. Make friends. Fill the shelves with poetry. Then when your books are on them, you'll be grateful for the Public Lending Right cheque that drops on the mat once a year. Libraries do more than lend books, CDs, records and cassettes, though the services they offer vary considerably; check what magazines they stock and ask for what you want; explore the range of on-screen information, the newsletters they produce; discover whether they promote readings, workshops, writers-in-residence or, as some counties do, a library-based literature festival.

Poetry Libraries

The specialist poetry libraries are also information centres invaluable to anyone who wants to keep tabs on the scene. The Arts Council of Great Britain founded the Poetry Library in London, now part of the South Bank Centre, in 1953. Philip Larkin called it 'one of the occasional pure flowerings of the imagination for which the English are so seldom given credit'. The Library is in the Royal Festival Hall, and membership is free. It houses all twentieth-century poetry in English, as well as poetry of earlier centuries translated into English by modern poets. Books are available for reference and for borrowing. As well as books, pamphlets, poemcards, posters and all the current magazines it can obtain, the Library carries audio and video cassettes. Noticeboards are full of news of events, including those at the Voice Box auditorium next door. Updated lists of competitions, magazines, publishers, bookshops, groups and workshops can be picked up, or will be sent free if you provide an A4 s.a.e.

The Scottish Poetry Library in Edinburgh is justly described as an international poetry resource centre. The emphasis is on twentieth-century work in Scots, Gaelic and English, but it houses an impressive collection of poetry in translation, especially from minority cultures. Information about events and resources is on display. A computerised catalogue and subject-index, INSPIRE, has been developed. There is a newsletter for paid-up members who can also use the reading-room with magazines for reference and audio-visual facilities for sound and video cassettes. The Library is spreading its net to include branches in Glasgow, Renfrew, Dundee, Inverness, Perth, Lerwick and Ullapool, and a travelling collection. Borrowing is free though there is a charge for postal loans.

The Austin Clarke Library, run by Poetry Ireland in Dublin, includes the poet's own collection of modern poetry, with the emphasis on Irish work. It disseminates information, publishes a newsletter, organises events and administers a postal book club (see below). Contact the librarian for information on membership.

The same applies to the Northern Arts Poetry Library in Morpeth. It has a collection of 6,000 books published since 1968 and its membership, who must live in the North East or Cumbria, can borrow books free by post. Oriel, the Welsh Arts Council's Bookshop in Cardiff, is a bookshop rather than a library, but as a resource for poets in Wales it plays a similar pivotal rôle.

Bookshops

If all the people who said they loved poetry bought it, the bookshops would stock more of it, publishers would be less nervous and poets would be richer. Establish a good relationship with your local bookshop. This is not done by whining that your poetry pamphlet isn't on the shelves, when you don't buy books there yourself. Shake, don't bite the hand that feeds. Ask for titles, order what's not in stock, and you'll gently educate the owner or manager about the range and excitement of contemporary poetry, and the professionalism of specialist poetry publishers. Many small presses market their books wholly or in part by mail order – if you follow the pointers in this book you'll find out about them – but bookshops are at the sharp end where poetry meets the public. Value them, buy from them, unless you'd rather see all the shelves in town stocked with videos.

Book Clubs

If you can't get to bookshops, and don't mind choices being made for you by a team of expert selectors, join the Poetry Book Society. Founded by T.S. Eliot in 1953, it offers four new books a year – the PBS Choices, a quarterly bulletin, an annual anthology, and the option of discounts on two dozen more books a year – the PBS Recommendations, Special Commendations and Recommended Translations, as well as other special offers, all post free. There is also a more expensive membership package which buys all the Choices and Recommendations. Poetry Ireland also runs a book club which picks four of the best books published in Ireland each year.

The vision of miles of shelves and acres of print out there, of magazines and books crashing through the letterbox, may still intimidate you. If you're new to the scene you can't take it all in at once. Follow your nose, but sniff widely in order to enlarge your taste; lead yourself to banquets you didn't think possible, for which you didn't realise you had an appetite.

If you feel, as you face these transmogrified mountains of tree-trunks and vats of ink, that it's all been done already, perhaps you should think again about writing. Think positively. In *The Anxiety of Influence*, the critic Harold Bloom takes an idiosyncratic look at literary history: the young poet, threatened by the past's crushing weight, challenges tradition in order to give himself air, allow herself vision. It's Oedipal: envious boy Wordsworth reveres daddy Milton but refuses to be emasculated by him; son Shelley writes 'Ode to the West Wind', a battling misreading of daddy Wordsworth's 'Ode: Intimations of Immortality', in order to grow up and away from his literary parent. It's worth thinking about. There's still work to be done after you've read all those books. Take advice from the seventeenth-century Japanese poet Matsuo Basho: 'Do not seek to follow in the footsteps of the men of old; seek what they sought.'

See Listings, pages 102 & 103.

CHAPTER FOUR

Voices

'Poetry, like music, is to be heard.' – BASIL BUNTING

'The ear does it. The ear is the only true writer and the only true reader.' – ROBERT FROST

Some people can sit down with a musical score and hear the music in their heads. They're lucky, I have to go to the performance or play the recording. But when I read a good poem, even if my lips don't move, I'm compelled to listen to it. I can't skim poetry. I must give it the time that its music takes.

A poem's score is implicit. It relies for its realisation on the reader's aural empathy with the writer's idiom. The length of the lines and the shape of the stanzas or of the whole poem on the page give the first clues. The number of syllables in the line, the pattern of stresses in it, the metre that builds the rhythm, these may create a tune characterised by regularity and recurrence; or they may open out, carried by the words' momentum, driven by the breath the line demands, pointed by the syllable's weight, bracketed or linked by pauses, by silence and space, moving to their own measure, growing like improvisation grows, or building into a large shape such as a fugue or a sonata. The pattern may be tight or loose, closed or open, but it will always depend on the tension between rhythm and diction, on how stress, tone and pitch complement the best words in the best order and the imagery they hold and will release. The idiom, the tune and the energy were once the writer's. Now they are the poem's. It waits to be played, to be turned on like a fountain or set off like a depth charge.

The poet's own reading of a poem isn't necessarily the best or most revealing one. Poets aren't always good performers, but their renderings are the nearest you can get to hearing the poem with the ear that wrote it. They reach back to the tradition of the makar, the bard, the troubadour. Readings give insights into the whole person who made the poems, who may be less important than the work, but whose presence and talk will be inspiring or salutary. At the least, you return from a reading with an ear more intimately attuned to the text.

The Circuit and the Circus

Writers' tours are organised by the Arts Councils, Regional Arts Boards, the Poetry Society, Poetry Ireland and others; one-off poetry readings are promoted by numerous writers' groups, arts centres, galleries, libraries and committed individuals who do so much to keep literature live; literature festivals provide a platform for a plethora of poets. If you don't know what's happening near you, ask your Regional Arts Board. Go and listen. Buy some signed books. Be horrified, be awestruck.

Some performers aim for the sure-fire: their poems are larded with stock phrases and belly-laughs for instant response; the live audience is their forum. Such performance poets should be seen and not read. Then there are poets who write to be read but also see readings as central to their rôle. Brian Patten, for instance, who was in part responsible for the revival of poetry as performance, expects his audience to come to an event in the same spirit they'd attend theatre. Michael Horovitz, anglo-saxophone and all, has been a catalyst for large-scale poetry and jazz marathons. Jean Binta Breeze tours successfully as an exponent of dub poetry, its roots in the reggae rhythm of twenty years ago, now increasingly flowering in print as well as performance. Kit Wright's jokes make us laugh, his wit and skill make us smile and his way of reaching deep into the dark, his and ours, moves us to tears. U.A. Fanthorpe radiates integrity and charm, with a cutting edge; her humour and depth please the head and warm or chill the heart. But there are also poets who deliver their work like a priest in a pulpit, or a solicitor reading a will at a wake. They may write like angels but they leave their wings at home when they go to face an audience; they simply cannot project themselves or their writing. But fortunately there are many who do excellent work on their feet as well as at their desks.

If you do your own readings, or plan to, you can learn a lot from listening and watching. A few nights ago I went to an event at an arts festival, billed in glowing terms as a reading by two brilliant poets. I hoped to make a happy discovery. One had a chair on the platform and sat down to read, partly hidden by a music stand. The other stood, off the platform, and leant against the back wall. The first introduced the evening with lengthy autobiographical applomb. The second added a few pleased remarks. The first read a poem, after a lecture on poetics. The second told us it was a great poem, and explained how it came to be that they, almost alone, maintained the Great Tradition. He read a short poem. His friend explained how profound it was, while flipping repeatedly through his self-published collected works, trying to locate his next offering...Friends from the audience hailed as Good Readers were asked to stand up and read some of the great men's works, whether they'd seen them before or not. The first man then rubbished a group of poets who'd read very professionally to a full house the night before, inveighing against lack of seriousness and advocating the re-use of that innovation of Gerard Manley Hopkins – whose poetry was incidentally not, ahem, valued by the Poet Laureate Bridges – that innovation, Sprung Rhyme (sic). And then he read us, was it his fourth poem of the evening?

It's not often I walk out of poetry readings. The world affords little enough money and glory to poets. Readings offer the chance of a little of each. They attract writers who preen and pose, who lean a bardic ego on their hearers with more or less effect. Fine writers also can become too busy with, and dependent upon the circuit; solid achievment recedes, new poems grow flimsier, charisma inflates; they need to give time back to themselves and their work, less to the audience. But I believe that poetry in performance is a life-giving, inspiring element of the scene. There are evenings that I want never to forget, and poets now dead whose books are tuned for me – scores as well as texts – because I recall their voices, their poise, their presence: Hugh MacDiarmid's passionate, vituperative, touching recital from *A Drunk Man Looks at the Thistle*; the strength and delicacy that Frances Horovitz, consummate performer, brought to her reading of lyrics like sensuous prayers, spare spells, mythic topography; Basil Bunting's voicing of *Briggflatts*, vigorous and rueful, stoical and almost serene.

Recordings and Broadcasting

Since Alfred Lord Tennyson laid down 'The Charge of the Light Brigade' in rolling Lincolnshire tones on a wax cylinder, poets have increasingly recorded their work. Performances are available on many labels; the Poetry Libraries have collections of records, cassettes and videos. The listener is not part of a live audience which creates the conditions for a performance, but can nevertheless witness a poet interpreting his or her own score. Or an actor interpreting a poet's music.

Actors are commonly damned for using poetry as a vehicle for enjoying the sound of their own voices, for thinking of poetry as an easy job, for leaving the poem with ego on its surface. This happens, but I've been lucky in working with several actors who have been willing to dig deep. I'll never forget meeting Maurice Denham before he was to record my *Poems of Z*; I was prepared to explore the sequence with him, to point up its development, its cross-references, its shifts of tone. I said, 'First, tell me how you see it.' And he did, better than I could have told him.

Radio should provide more opportunities for poets. While BBC Radio 3 has reduced its poetry output (dropping both *Poetry Now* and *Poet of the Month*), Radio 4 still runs its popular series *Poetry Please*, and has replaced its long-running *Time for Verse* with a new series called *Stanza*. Radio 5 has *Talking Poetry*, aimed at children but absorbing listening for anyone, as well as two schools poetry programmes, *Poetry Corner* and *Verse Universe*. Radios 3 and 4 also have occasional poetry features, and there are sometimes poetry slots on general arts programmes like *Kaleidoscope*. In Ireland there are several arts and literature programmes on RTE radio and television which feature poets, the best known being *The Arts Show*; *The Poet's Voice* on RTE Radio 1 is an interview and readings series, and there are two new Radio 1 poetry slots, a books programme presented by Theo Dorgan and a poetry programme fronted by Mary O'Donnell. This list may suggest that there is a lot of poetry on the radio, but there isn't. So do write and ask the BBC, RTE or your local stations for more. Praise a programme you've enjoyed and suggest what you'd like to hear. A few letters are strong medicine to producers and programme controllers.

Television is more problematical. Tony Harrison's poetry-films (like v., *The Blasphemers' Banquet* and *The Gaze of the Gorgon*) are tough and exciting, and the latter's producer Peter Symes is pioneering refreshing new approaches to television poetry, most recently with his *Words on Film* series. But too often producers faced with poetry, and the problem of applying images to it, affect a deadening "poetic" style; we get readers in Rembrandt-light or set in some puritan-stark cell; poets wander in cornfields, or stand gazing into the sea. Why poetry brings all the filmic clichés tumbling out of the director's bag, and why poets allow the audience to be alienated by such suicidal preciousness, I can't explain.

Recordings and broadcasts are the media version of the oral tradition. They add to the richness of our experience of poetry and are indispensable to visually-handicapped listeners. For most of us they, like live readings, lead back to the page. A poet or an actor reading aloud must choose one route through a text, only hinting at deliberate ambiguities, only playing one tune, one variation. With a tuned ear we can return to the printed poem to discover its scope and to fit our own breath to its score.

CHAPTER FIVE

Riches

'Poetry...is a bit like mining. One day you strike, and strike
the rock, and nothing happens; the next, you hit it, and
extract silver.' – EAVAN BOLAND

'Poets evermore are scant of gold.'
– ELIZABETH BARRETT BROWNING

Poetry and money. If you've turned to this chapter first, I suggest
you go back and start at the beginning of the book. This is a very
short chapter. If you know how a poet can make a fortune out of
poetry please write to me without delay. Poetry and money are
mutually exclusive. Almost.

Is this a cold douche you could do without? I'm sorry, but publishers and others in the poetry business assure me that they con-
tinually come across people who are convinced that once they get
published they can give up work or come off the dole, retire to
the south of Utopia or buy a castle in the air.

We all need money, but if you need money as proof of success
you'll never succeed as a poet. You must write because you value
the process of writing and because, at least some of the time, you
value the finished product. Your sense of its value is confirmed
when someone who reads it says *Yes!* This is all very noble. It's
equally true that we like to be valued, we value the self-affirmation
a little acclaim brings, we love the attention. Poets are human too.

In the ideal republic poets should be rewarded with more than
a warm glow for the hard work they do. But only a handful can
earn a living from their poetry, and most of those from performing
rather than publishing it. Those of us who are freelance writers
earn money if we're lucky from other kinds of writing – reviewing,
journalism, novels, genre fiction, travel writing, biography, radio
and television. Many of us take up residencies, teach courses and
give readings and lectures. Some won't sell out; everything depends
on the poetry; they'll die first, like Martin Bell, in poverty. Most
sensible poets do proper jobs, if there's one to be had, and draw a
wage or a salary. There is, I'm told, such a thing as a sensible poet.

Amateurs and Professionals

A good poet is an amateur who behaves like a professional. That sounds like someone who has a hobby and thinks he should be paid for it, or one who lacks skill and judgement but makes a career of it all the same. You may think there are poets in both categories, but I'm thinking of earlier meanings of the words: amateur – one who does something for love; professional – one who professes and pursues a vocation. This is all very noble, and I'm not apologising for that.

Someone who loves what they do wants it to be loved. The first step is to get your poems published in magazines. Chapter 7 deals with publishing in some detail. All I want to point out now is that though there are hundreds of periodicals that print poems, few pay for them, and very few pay a decent rate. You get a free copy or two, or £3, or £30 plus if you're lucky.

These rewards are yours when you get a poem accepted and printed. The fact is that even the small press magazines publish a minute proportion of the poems they are sent. Some say less than 1%, some up to 5%. The competition is enormous. If you'd didn't value what you do, you wouldn't keep on trying.

And would it have been worth it, after all, after the stamps, rejection slips, the tears...? Which brings me to books, and T.S. Eliot's old desk at Faber & Faber. Twenty or thirty manuscripts get as far as the present poetry editor's office every week. His predecessor took on six new (to Faber) poets in eleven years. Bloodaxe Books published first collections by forty poets in the same period, with fifty to sixty manuscripts a week to choose from. The percentages are almost too depressing to work out. 0.1% for Oxford University Press, one new poet a year. The point is made, and is echoed on publishers' desks everywhere.

And how much would your book earn in royalties? Publishers used to be pleased if they sold 500. It was worthy, respectable, genteel to have a poetry list. Work out 10% of the selling-price on 500 copies. You can do a lot with £200 or so, you could even buy a few books.

So, we're talking worth, value, poetic riches; we're not talking money. We will, of course, since we're professionals. But first, let's get our priorities right. I said it would be a short chapter.

CHAPTER SIX

Winning Words

'What is required is simply the masterpiece we'd all write if we could.
There is only one prescription for it: it's got to be good.'
 — FLEUR ADCOCK

'This miserable bartering of fame, this coveting of it, fighting for
it, tearing it from mouth to mouth... this continual talking about
literature in ignorance as if it were some sort of commerce...'
 — GIACOMO LEOPARDI

A handful of poems in any one year earn far more than a few pounds.
Every other year one is worth £5,000. It's judged to be so, at any
rate. It's the first prize-winner in the Arvon International Poetry
Competition which began in 1980. Top prize in the Poetry Society's
National Poetry Competition is £4,000; in the Peterloo Poets Open
Poetry Competition it's £3,000. Others – such as the City of Cardiff
International Poetry Competition and the Welsh Academy's John
Tripp Award for Spoken Poetry – offer first prizes of £1,000.

Competitions arouse strong feelings. Lust for money and fame,
for instance. Disgust at the vulgarity that taints high art. Delight
that for once poetry has a chance of making news, making the air-
waves, being seen to be the popular form that it is – among writers if not readers. Concern that the "event" may receive more cov-
erage than the poetry. Cynicism that it is just one more symptom
of late capitalist media-ocrity. Scepticism that a great poem will
almost certainly be overlooked by judges who are bogged down in
a welter of entries. Criticism that they are stuck in a middle-of-
the-road tradition, and are probably jealous and spiteful too. Anxiety
that where a number of judges are at work, the "consensus poem"
will win. Anger that when there's one judge the choice will be idiosyncratic. Suspicion that judges will recognise and reward the work
of their friends. Fear of losing.

In general competitions are well and fairly run. I suspect that the
best poems usually win, if there can be agreement about what a best
poem is – that is, they usually pick up the top prizes, although the
best single poem may not always win first prize. But isn't it a bit
like vanity publishing, the incompetent paying for an illusory chance
of glory? At least the few who profit from the vain multitude are

poets. I'm all for money being put in the pockets of poets, whether winners or judges, and don't much care whether it comes from the pockets of the mass of entrants or from a competition's commercial sponsors. I can debate with myself for a long time. You decide; you may choose to enter them because they're there.

But some 'competitions' are scams and are multiplying alarmingly. You answer an advert asking for poems, then get a reply from the Bards Council of Great Britain or whatever grandiose name they've given themselves: apparently you've reached the next round and they want permission to print your poem in an anthology available to lucky you, at a cost. For a further payment they may include a biographical note. Beware!

Each year there are mutterings that the poetry competition bonanza has boomed and bust, and each year there seem to be more. There's one for haiku or senryu, one for Christian poetry, for poems on the rainforest, poems that celebrate the New Age, poems that rhyme in traditional forms or otherwise, innovative poems, poems by the under 16s or over 18s, by Northern writers, by poets of Afro-Caribbean or Asian origin, by authors of love lyrics or of the very best poem entitled 'The Unfortunate Kazoo'.

Competitions are run by by local arts societies such as Bridport, by literature festivals like Cheltenham, by publishers, bookshops, magazines and newspapers. Some have substantial sponsors and offer big prizes, some guarantee a percentage of the take, while others offer publication in an anthology or magazine as the reward. The Poetry Business Competition is one that offers publication – in one volume of the best two 16-page collections of poems submitted. The entry fee for that is currently £10. The rest charge between £1 and £5 per poem.

If you decide that that sort of money is a good investment, find out what competitions are currently inviting entries. The bigger ones are listed in the *Writers' and Artists' Yearbook*; an updated selective list is available from the Poetry Library in London if you send an A4 s.a.e.; your Regional Arts Board, its magazine or newsletter will tell you about local ones; and the literary press carries many advertisements. The conditions of entry vary enormously, so always write to each competition with an s.a.e. for an entry form. Abide by the rules, pay your money and let them take their choice.

The judges are usually poets of some reputation, editors or, in the case of one 1991 competition, Ronnie Corbett. Whether they are judging funny poems or not, it's hard for judges to retain a sense of humour in the face of hundreds or thousands of poems; as a rule they are extraordinarily conscientious and certainly earn their fees. It is sadly true that 90% or more of the submissions are dropped on the reject pile without any qualms; it's clear that however well-intentioned the writer is, however authentic the idea, feeling or experience that stimulated the work, it has failed to harness language and imagination. It's usually obvious that the would-be poet does not read poetry or bother to understand it. So far so bad. It's the poems that are sifted on to the possible and probable piles that cause the headaches until – and many judges testify to this – until one slides unobtrusively out of the heap and smacks them, dries the back of the throat, makes the heart stall: it's luminous, authentic and well-made. A judge who finds one is fortunate. Phew! it's going to be one of the winners.

As epigraph to this chapter I chose two lines from a poem by Fleur Adcock. Here it is in full:

The Prize-Winning Poem

It will be typed, of course, and not all in capitals: it will use upper and
    lower case
in the normal way; and where a space is usual it will have a space.
It will probably be on white paper, or possibly blue, but almost certainly
    not pink.
It will not be decorated with ornamental scroll-work in coloured ink,
nor will a photograph of the poet be glued above his or her name,
and still less a snap of the poet's children frolicking in a jolly game.
The poem will not be about feeling lonely and being fifteen
and unless the occasion of the competition is a royal jubilee it will not be
    about the queen.
It will not be the first poem the author has written in his life
and will probably not be about the death of his daughter, son or wife
because although to write such elegies fulfils a therapeutic need
in large numbers they are deeply depressing for the judges to read.
The title will not be 'Thoughts' or 'Life' or 'I Wonder Why'
or 'The Bunny-rabbit's Birthday Party' or 'In Days of Long Gone By'.
'Tis and 'twas, o'er and e'er, and such poetical contractions will not be
    found
in the chosen poem. Similarly clichés will not abound:
dawn will not herald another bright new day, nor dew sparkle like
    diamonds in a dell,
nor trees their arms upstretch. Also the poet will be able to spell.
Large meaningless concepts will not be viewed with favour: myriad is out;
infinity is becoming suspect, aeons and galaxies are in some doubt.
Archaisms and inversions will not occur; nymphs will not their fate bemoan.
Apart from this there will be no restrictions upon the style or tone.
What is required is simply the masterpiece we'd all write if we could.
There is only one prescription for it: it's got to be good.

What if you win? Well, there's that momentary mad sensation that you've written the best poem in the universe and it's been recognised. The pure outpouring of your genius has been translated into filthy lucre. It will probably be published. It may be broadcast. Editors and publishers and your sister-in-law will take notice and want to see what else you've written. Some previously unknown winners have had their first collections snapped up by publishers shortly afterwards, for example Medbh McGuckian and David Scott. In Andrew Motion's case, his £5,000 prize was the cue for media stardom. Listen to the whispered warning in your ear against hubris, but be glad that you've made it a rung or two up the poets' rickety apology for a career structure. And hope that tomorrow you'll be able to write one as good again.

Awards and Bursaries

'We symbolically join here in refusing the terms of patriarchal competition and declaring that we will share this prize among us, to be used as best we can for women.' So poetry prizewinner Adrienne Rich joined in a statement with nominees Audre Lord and Alice Walker at the 1974 U.S. National Book Awards. She rejected her award, they accepted it in the name of all women, 'the silent women whose voices have been denied us, the articulate women who have given us strength to do our work'.

It was a strong feminist statement; they put their prize-money where their mouths were. They would not be bought and tamed by the literary establishment. It's a hard thing for poets to turn down money, and a powerful gesture. Others think they should grab any crumbs society brushes in their direction.

Most awards and bursaries are for writers with a body of work under their belts. They are administered by Arts Councils, some Regional Arts organisations, the Society of Authors, the Poetry Society, independent trusts, educational and other bodies. The Irish Arts Council supports a unique academy of outstanding artists, Aosdána; a number of its members are granted a stipend, or Cnuas, of £5,500 per annum for five years; twenty-one of them are poets.

There are many awards for which your publisher can apply once you've had a book published, including the Forward Poetry Prizes for Best Collection (£10,000) and Best First Collection (£5,000), the Poetry Book Society's T.S. Eliot Prize (£5,000), and the £2,000 Whitbread Poetry Award – whose winner could become Whitbread Book of the Year (£21,000). There are also grants given on the basis of your past work's quality for what you plan to do next: they buy time, pay for childcare, enable you to travel, nurture you as a poet.

The Writers' and Artists' Yearbook sets out the criteria for a range of awards, and the Book Trust's *A Guide to Literary Prizes, Grants and Awards in Britain and Ireland* is as near comprehensive a listing as possible. A number are for as yet unpublished writers. Eligibility for them may depend upon your nationality, your age and where you live. Criteria for awards from publicly funded arts organisations vary enormously from region to region and from year to year. Arts Boards and Associations have in general moved towards supporting community development projects which may involve writers, rather than giving money to individuals; some fund publishers' lists, others give grants towards a particular title; a few still give bursaries direct to writers who have had at least some work published in magazines or anthologies. Because arts funding policy is in a continual state of flux, you must contact the officer responsible for literature in your area and find out exactly what is flavour of the month.

An award which has encouraged many young poets and often led to book publication is administered by the Society of Authors: if you're under thirty and were born and are resident in the U.K. or Northern Ireland you can submit work for an Eric Gregory Award. Perhaps too many awards are for young rather than new writers. If you're a late starter because you've brought up a family, or because that's how you are, it's tough that so many literary baubles are reserved for the under forties. For poets there should be an equivalent to the McKitterick Prize of £5,000 for a first novel by an author over the age of forty. A number of notable literary lives have begun about then.

If you scan the lists of past recipients of, for example, the Somerset Maugham, Cholmondeley, Denis Devlin Memorial, Patrick Kavanagh, Eric Gregory and Alice Hunt Bartlett Awards, or of bursaries from the Arts Councils, it's clear that many fine poets – and some who've sunk without trace – have been encouraged and, in some cases, helped to survive, by both privately endowed trusts and public money. You may nevertheless feel that it's a closed shop. It's not. The names of the prizewinning poets may be familiar now, but they often weren't when the awards were made. Doors aren't always thrown as wide as they should be, but if you apply appropriately there's every chance that a prize, an award, a grant or a bursary could justify your faith in your work. Of course, as the poet said, it's got to be good.

See also Listings, pages 102 & 103.

CHAPTER SEVEN

Put to Bed

'Oh that my words were now written! oh that they were
printed in a book!' – JOB

'I have come to the conclusion that this country is entirely
inhabited by unpublished minor poets.' – JOHN HEATH-STUBBS

Dear Sir/Madam,

I found your address in the Writers and Artists Year Book, so I
thought I'd submit to you. I write poetry as a hobby and all my
freinds think it is very good, and that I should have it published.
It is not often that I have sent my work to anyone, so please do me
the kindness of perusing what I have sent. Most of the so-called
poetry published nowadays isn't what I'd call Poetry, and everyone tells me that my verses are. If your an editor of real taste I feel
you'll want to publish me.

My poetry may not be the fashionable sort but it's what the public wants to read if they were asked. I'm a great believer in tried
and tested ways of using words and I have little patience with the
latest Poetic Fads. I have sent you a small selection. I wrote the
first 50 poems in the Manuscript during the past month. The one's
at the back are older, going back to last year. The folded one's
which are seperate are very new, and I only finished two of them
this morning.

You will see that most of the poems here are about Nature and
my feelings for my late wife Marilyn, who died last year of a heart
condition and complications I won't go into now. I have also written poems about a range of topics, including whales, the Environ-
ment, modern soceity, Football Hooligans, God and 'Things That
Children Say'. If you'd prefer other subjects please let me know
what you would like.

I would be willing to offer you the First British Serial Rights on
my poems ON THE STRICT UNDERSTANDING THAT MY
POEMS REMAIN MY COPYRIGHT and you cannot publish them
without my permission. As you see, my Solicitor and my Bank Manager have sertified that these poems are my own original work and
noone elses. How much are you willing to pay? If you're rate is too
low I may decide to consult a literary agent and ask him to act.

If for some reason you aren't able to publish my Work, I would be grateful if you could give me some critical response and tell me what are their good or bad points. I really would very much value your honest professional opinion and therefore hope for something more helpful than the Rejection Slip. Also, if you can suggest any other Magazines or Publisher's to which I should submit, please give me their addresses.

I am inclined to think that Poetry is a closed shop where its 'who you know' that matters. How else is it that so much bad poetry is published while true quality gets ignored. But I hope you will be able to prove that some Editors know true poetry when they read it, and will want to publish me, otherwise my life will not be worth living because I firmly beleive that my Work is good enough to be read by Posterity and in schools.

Yours in anticipation,   DUFF WORDSMITH.

Is this letter an outrageous send-up? Editors everywhere will recognise it. It's a mild example, almost bland. It's not nearly as desperately pleading as many that they receive. Duff's spelling is not *too* bad. He does not explicitly threaten suicide. Many such letters name the 'rubbish' that the editor has previously published; Duff is more circumspect. He is quite sane and does not put kisses at the bottom. There is no claim to the Truth, or to possession of the poetical panacea for the spiritual decline of civilisation. It seems that he is not a medium, nor does a ouija board write the poems. Duff is relatively modest and cannot presume to deliver a lecture in immaculate prose on the corruption of the literary establishment, or on the unjustly neglected poets to whom he is heir. He is not purging the language single-handed. He does not claim to represent a post-post-modernist poetic school. Neither his letter nor his verses are stuffed with four-letter claims to credibility. And his next letter, in rapid response to the note on the rejection slip, will not promise a libel action, will not be a packet of shit, will not threaten the editor with physical violence.

Some do. Bear this in mind when you offer work to editors. Be merciful, or at least straightforward. Be brief and let the poems speak for themselves; a long letter is a sure sign they can't. Try imagining yourself into the editor's chair: he or she can publish perhaps 2% of what comes through the post, is always hard-pressed, probably part-time, often underpaid, or unpaid and doing the job out of belief in the possibilities of poetry. The editor is dedicated to offering a platform to poets, a species supposed to be strong on imagination and empathy. *Not*, the editor thinks, *when it comes to me.*

Magazines

'O blatant Magazines, regard me rather –
Since I blush to belaud myself a moment –
As some rare little rose, a piece of inmost
Horticultural art...' – TENNYSON

So, you're still determined to get your poems put to bed. If you want to see your name on the spine of a book, first establish a track record in the magazines. If you're serious you'll already be subscribing to some, or getting hold of them somehow. Find out which magazines print work you like. Send to them. You'll only waste time and stamps otherwise. Editors' policies and sensibilities vary enormously, but they all agree on one thing: that would-be contributors should read a magazine before sending work to it. It's not wise to send poems suitable for *Agenda* to *Joe Soap's Canoe*. On the other hand, poems that *Joe Soap's Canoe* would accept might also interest *Slow Dancer*.

Until you've read these magazines closely, there's not much point knowing that one ploughs a broadly modernist furrow while another professes a post-modernist, New York School leaning. Some editors promote a particular genre or group because they think that's where the future lies. Others are more catholic, not because they hedge their bets but because they believe in poetry's variousness. *Verse*, for instance, invites any genuinely contemporary original poetry in English, Scots or Gaelic with parallel English text. *Iron*'s editor responds to variety but tries to avoid the obscure, the over-academic and the incestuous. 'Spectacular failure sometimes beats safe success,' he says. Another poetry editor wants work that is excited about experience, and welcomes formal poems while acknowledging that good ones are rare; she looks for both clarity and mystery among the layers of meaning. She loathes moral superiority: 'It is Great Thoughts that need to be silenced.'

All editors want to see original work. "Original" means not imitative; editors get tired of reading more or less the same poems over and over again, especially when they've already been written better by Thomas Wyatt, S.T. Coleridge or Anne Stevenson. But "original" means much more than novel or fashionable or ahead of the fashion. Your original poem has its origin in you, you sparked by stimuli from within or without, you carrying the impulse to the paper and shaping it, tuning it there with as much art as you like. Your talent is yours by birth, your sensibility is at least partly earned, your craftsmanship is learned. In practice these become indivisible. Will you understand me when I say that once you are working responsibly you can make choices, and once these are made you have no choice? You write as you must. You may be free to borrow and steal from other writers, but you're on the road to originality. The work is true to its origin, it's authentic. It's as different as you are. It may be strikingly novel.

Submission

Editors want original work and they want it in an envelope which hasn't disintegrated, with a stamp that covers the postage. They want it accompanied by a stamped addressed envelope, preferably big enough to contain the poems. It is an advantage if the poems are legibly typed. Forgive me for stating what's obvious to you. Exasperated editors bear witness to the number of contributors to whom such professional behaviour is obviously alien.

Unless your poems are "concrete" ones they should be typed, in black on one side of white medium-weight A4 paper. Photocopies (legible) are perfectly acceptable, as are sheets or printouts from a word-processor (as long as the ribbon is still capable of producing clear black type). They should look near as dammit as you want them printed. Poetry, unlike prose, does not need to be double-spaced. Sultry or bardic snapshots of yourself should not be attached to them, nor should they be decorated with flowers or runes. Each poem however short should have a sheet to itself. If it takes up more than one page, or is part of a sequence, each sheet should be named and numbered. Every sheet should bear your name and address.

Submit more than one poem, but not your life's work. Send four or half a dozen out at a time, held together with a paperclip not a staple, an s.a.e. – or a self-addressed envelope with an international reply coupon from the post office if you're sending abroad or from abroad – and a brief letter. Address it to the editor by name. Don't be stiff and chilly. Don't gush. Don't write your autobiography or a treatise on poesy. Simply ask that your poems be considered for publication. If you've won a prize you might mention it – a prize for poetry that is; don't go on about your sub-aqua medals or your Ph.D. You could quote a review you've had in a good periodical, but don't list all the tiny magazines that have printed your work or the readings you've given to poetry groups. Don't blow your own trumpet, the poems themselves must do that. If they come back with a rejection slip, be ready to post them straight off to the next magazine. Rejection is not pleasant. Self-pity can paralyse. Act at once and, when the manuscript looks dog-eared or otherwise dog-tired, type or print out crisp copies.

Keep a record of when and where you have submitted which poems. Always keep copies of your work.

Some editors are speedy and some are very slow. After three months it's quite acceptable to ask after your poems' fate, but don't besiege them, don't abuse them or come the prima-donna. If you're rejected, don't fling the same poems back screaming that they're unjustly-spurned masterpieces. Don't start a war. When you get more than a rejection slip, think yourself lucky. Take note of criticism: it may not be gospel but it's almost always useful. If the editor suggests changes in a poem, see whether you agree; if you can change it, send it back. A well-known editor once wrote to say that a poem of mine interested him but needed drastic pruning. I did what I could: I changed a semi-colon to a comma. Wonderful, he replied, we'll print it. Now I think I should have changed more. Enough said.

Poets are human; editors see the same frailties again and again. Almost all complain of abstraction; poets, however spiritual, know that poetry is rooted in the real world, the concrete, and that the specific has more chance of universal meaning than any amount of generalisation; as David Jones wrote, 'the works of man, unless they are of "now" and of "this place", can have no "for ever".' A poet may be intoxicated with words, but not blind drunk. Vision is too often blurred by repetition, tautology, periphrasis, circumlocution …Poetry needs not big words, but small ones used magically. Editors also wish would-be poets could spell, or at least bother to consult a dictionary.

Editors are human. They're wary immediately they see tell-tale signs of unprofessionalism in the way work is submitted. They're not always right, but they develop a nose for what they like. Your latest brilliant poem may be the hundredth like it they've seen in a month. They don't want to see any more called 'Hope' or 'Despair'; they're worn down by angst-ridden, self-referential love poetry; they grow to detest the view from the scullery window or moans about loneliness in bedsits by the seaside; both Greek gods and male drunk-on-dole poets' sexual exploits and/or fantasies grow tedious; dead right on socio-political poems about class and hospitals closing are usually, well, dead; 'Autumn at Newstead Abbey' and explicit sadism pall. There are literally hundreds of unpublished poems out there with the same title: 'At Sylvia Plath's Grave'. So they tell me. But if any one of those subjects was treated with originality – with feeling, wit, inventiveness – there's a good chance they might love it. And print the poem.

Books

' 'Tis pleasant, sure, to see one's name in print;
A book's a book, although there's nothing in't.' – BYRON

Every day presses place advertisements in papers and magazines begging poems for 'a prestigious anthology' and appealing to Authors and Poets for book-length manuscripts. 'Your book published!' This will strike you as odd; if you didn't already know, you now have some idea of the number of manuscripts that publishers receive and reject. When supply so far exceeds demand no publisher needs to advertise.

Sometimes these adverts list a few of the best-sellers and classics once rejected by publishers. There are plenty of good stories that provoke a sour, comforting guffaw in any would-be writer's wizened breast. 'Don't let this happen to you,' the adverts say, quite forgetting to add that all the spurned titles they mention were published sooner or later by reputable houses and made them and their authors a great deal of money.

These publishers make money from, rather than for, their authors. They are interested in your wallet not your work. They advertise to bring unpublished books in, but not to sell them when they're printed. They are not stigmatised as Vanity Presses for nothing. Their trade is flattery. They praise your talent, your poems, your judgment. They take your money and print your work, sometimes beautifully, leather-bound and gold-embossed if you pay extra. They market a little bit of immortality.

It's illusory. Libraries won't buy the books. Periodicals won't review them. The only shelves they adorn are yours, unless you get out there and tout them yourself. In the world of books your reputation can only suffer from vanity publication. You pay for self-esteem and are despised for it. It's worse than worthless. At best, it's a very expensive way of getting poems printed.

Printing is not publication. The word *publication* means to make public, to offer for public distribution or sale. If you want your work published go to a publisher. There are all kinds of vanity variants: presses or 'publishers' which offer 'co-partnership publication' (sic) or 'subsidy publication'; a few promise you a co-operative rather than an exploitative deal. One of these exceptions is Outposts Publications, founded by the late Howard Sergeant (and kept alive by Hippopotamus Press); it produces a magazine and a series of booklets, chosen for their quality, which do get reviewed; the backlist contains some well-respected names who were willing to subsidise and distribute their first publications. There are other players in this controversial area. My advice is, don't pay. But if you choose to subsidise your book, check exactly what you're getting in return.

Self-publication is a different matter. There's a long tradition of writers doing it – William Blake, Walt Whitman, Ezra Pound, Ian Hamilton Finlay and many more – that somehow makes it acceptable. Some writers do it to repudiate commercialism. Some like the exhilaration of the alternative. Some are impatient with publishers' slowness and do it themselves to get the beauty of it hot. For some, hands-on quality and freedom in design and execution are all important. Some produce finely-bound limited editions on hand-made paper; others run off duplicated, stapled pamphlets. You choose from all the means available and master those you need, or pay for your book to be printed and bound. Getting a finished book in your hands is the easy part. Getting if off your hands is more difficult. Publications in *Listings* will point you in the right direction, all the way from design to distribution. The risks are all yours, and the profits.

Community publishing is a lively option; the Federation of Worker Writers and Community Publishers stands against the élitist notion of English Literature and for the communal value of writing and production. If you feel you could contribute to this movement, find out from your regional arts board whether there's a group near you, like Bristol Broadsides or Hackney's Centreprise, or work towards founding one yourself. Self-publication or community-publication can be a good option for writers who are in a position to shift a reasonable number of books, where there is sufficient interest in the local community in a book by a "local writer" or where the work itself is of local interest.

If you have to pay to have your book produced, it is *considerably* cheaper to pay a printer for a straight printing job than it is to pay a vanity publisher for doing exactly the same work, the printing of copies of a book, but under the guise of "publication". The growth of "desk-top publishing" means that the typesetting and design part of book production can be done more easily by more people and more cheaply; it also means that the vanity publishers can make even bigger profits in charging you to produce your book. If you use a word-processor, most printers will offer a reduced price for printing the book if you let them have a copy of your text on disk. If you have access to a laser printer, you may even be able to print off proof copies which are adequate in quality for the printer to use without the need for any typesetting.

Big publishers and small presses

Most poets want to write poems. And have them published by as prestigious a publisher as possible. If you've built up a list of credits in magazines, it may be time to put a book together. But don't be in too much of a hurry. Don't be in a hurry. Don't hurry. I could fill a page with those words and an impatient poet would take no notice. Still, I've said it three times and that makes me feel I've done my job.

A bum poem in a magazine soon gets mislaid. To those with cruelly sharp memories you can say of the ones you'd rather forget, that they were written, like Shakespeare's plays, by someone else of the same name. A book sticks around. You want it to, but not when it enshrines a fully paid-up, pink-cheeked, sweaty embarrassment. So take your time.

Read old and new poetry voraciously. Look at publishers' lists. Assess plenty of published books; see which work, which don't and why. Choose fifty of your poems, or enough to make a book of 64 pages. Give it a good title: one that's appropriate to your collection and striking in isolation, or rather printed on one of many spines on a bookshop shelf. If you call it *The Meaningful Muse* the publisher's editor will yawn. Don't be pretentious or "poetic". If it works, use the title or a phrase from one of the best poems in the book. Be patient, let the title rise to the top.

Take care with the dedication. If you want one, it will be heartfelt, but keep it simple: 'To David' is better than 'To precious Daniel, my inspiration, who selflessly shared the joys and sufferings that were the genesis of these poems' or 'To darling Wumpy my constant companion throughout ten years of bardolotry, and he's only the dog'. Sentimental or whimsical dedications are instant emetics. Then come the Acknowledgements: a list of magazines, newspapers, radio programmes etc where the poems have appeared. These give credit where it's due and, for an editor to whom your name is new, are your credentials too. Then come the poems. Arrange them carefully. Play with the order. Find the best shape for the book. Leave it for a while, then return to it and gauge its impact. Don't be in a hurry to type the Contents page.

Take care over presentation. Go for clarity and simplicity: no precious bindings, just a bundle of well-typed, well-ordered poems with your name and address on the first and last sheets. If possible, show the book to a reader, or a writers' group, whose judgment you respect. Only when you're very sure it's ready, slip it into a folder, labelled with the title and your name, and send it off with a straightforward letter and s.a.e. to a publisher whose list of poets you know and like.

Houses that publish poetry come in all shapes and sizes. After a period of pessimism when some major publishers cut poetry altogether and others had dull declining lists, the last decade or so has seen a flowering of possibilities, stimulated by risk-taking innovative new publishers and the success of the big competitions. Gone are the days when the big names published verse on the side because it was a worthy thing to do. The gentility which both benefited and castrated poetry has given way to hype – more exciting, especially for the hypee, but just as dangerous. Commercial publishing will continue in flux while the epidemic of takeovers and their repercussions lasts. The most recent round of changes has resulted in the poetry lists at Chatto, Hutchinson, Secker and Sinclair-Stevenson being axed, so check that you're sending your book to a publisher that still exists, has the name it used to have and still maintains a poetry list. If in doubt, ring the switchboard, ask for the poetry editor's name.

Remember that big ones – such as Faber, Oxford University Press and Cape – take on very few new poets, and that Penguin take on none (their poetry books are mostly paperback reprints or selections from other publishers' books). In a recent newspaper interview Christopher Reid, poetry editor of Faber & Faber, said: 'If this article prompts people to send their work in, then all to the good.' Specialist poetry publishers would surely be pleased if the big houses took more risks themselves, rather than poaching poets once their names have been made by others (and with much hard graft).

Jacqueline Simms, poetry editor (part-time) of Oxford University Press, says that only 10% of collections submitted are full-length (say 30-plus poems) and seriously eligible. They are the ones that get past her assistant or reader and onto her desk. Of those maybe 1% get published. Very seldom will they arrive totally out of the blue, from wholly unknown writers.

New voices can find a platform in anthologies such as Faber's *Poetry Introduction* series. Some of the specialists do the same: Peterloo Poets' *Peterloo Preview*, Anvil Press's *Anvil New Poets*, and introduction anthologies from Seren, Arc, Blackstaff and Flambard. These are stepping-stones to an individual collection, though inclusion in *Poetry Introduction*, for example, by no means guarantees a place on Faber's list.

Carcanet Press produces its own eclectic mix of poets, while Bloodaxe Books has ploughed a broad and vigorous furrow, between the dry and dusty and the wild and woolly, and now brings out more poetry and more new poets than any other publisher. Peterloo, Arc, Enitharmon and Flambard are increasingly impressive and, as always, some of the liveliest and most ambitious work issues from so-called small or little presses, such as Headland, Rockingham, Smith/Doorstop and Stride, and from Allardyce Barnett, Pig Press, Spectacular Diseases and Street Editions, four of the leading imprints with a special interest in Modernist, Post-Modernist and experimental poetry. In Ireland the Gallery Press has a distinguished list including many leading Irish poets as well as new writers, while Blackstaff, Dedalus and Salmon publish most other Irish poets of any note (apart from those published from Britain).

A selection of big and small publishers, including some catering for specialist tendencies and interest groups, is included in *Listings*. The choice is enormous, and it's yours. When you've made it and sent off your book, all you can do is wait. Some poets wait three days before ringing up to ask if it's going to be published. Don't. If you get rejected within ten days don't assume that your work hasn't been read. Some publishers try to read everything fast and only retain those manuscripts that need further consideration. They're doing you a favour if they're able to return your work promptly. Don't expect a critical analysis of your work: publishers aren't there to provide a free critical service. You're asking them to say whether or not they will publish your work; with the volume of submissions they receive, it's not possible for them to write explanatory letters when returning all the books they are unable or unwilling to publish. If you haven't heard after three months, enquire. Don't send the manuscript to more than one place at a time. It's bad practice; in any case, your least favourite publisher might say yes first; and if you get caught out a reputation for two-timing will do you no good at all.

When your favourite publisher says yes, have a few drinks and thank your muse. Then ask for a contract. Don't worry about copyright; that's yours unless you sign it away. Dylan Thomas once did. Don't. The publisher does not acquire your copyright, but controls certain publication rights to it under terms which you agree while the book is kept in print; the copyright remains yours throughout. Check the contract carefully. It should stipulate that your book will be published within a reasonable period of time and at an agreed approximate price. See that it promises you 10% royalties and regular statements (7.5% on bulk and export sales is also usual). Get an advance if you can. Make sure that rights cannot be assigned by the publisher without your permission. If the book is not reprinted, rights should revert to you no later than twelve months after it sells out. If the book is remaindered you should have first offer of copies at the remainder price. If you have an agent, let them worry. Otherwise, professional bodies like the Society of Authors or the Writers' Guild offer legal advice to members. I suggest you get the contract vetted even if the publisher insists that it's the standard one that every author gets. A contract works both ways: it's your agreement with the publisher as well as vice versa. Get it right. Moments of triumph should not end in tears.

You've put all you can into your poems, all your passion and fury and craft. You've tried to keep your feelings out of the letters to editors, out of the business of getting rejected or published. You haven't of course, but you've certainly wasted them on editors who don't like your work, and found that it's wise to be cool and businesslike with those who do. But when your first book comes out, celebrate immoderately in the way you like best. Don't be coy or staid. You've got a book out in the world! There's never another moment like it.

See Listings, pages 106-110.

CHAPTER EIGHT

Paranoia

'Why – do they shut Me out of Heaven?
Did I sing – too loud?' – EMILY DICKINSON

'Most critics are men who have not had much luck and who,
just about the time they were growing desperate, found a quiet
little job as cemetery watchmen.' – JEAN-PAUL SARTRE

The more exclusive the sect, the more expansive its demonology. Poets, like other artists, like other human beings, are very good at colonising high ground. The atmosphere is rarefied, the peaks – piques – are sharp; poets are not medieval angels, not many can dance on a pin's point without puncturing their metrical feet. Each group of the elect expends energy trying to prove it squats on the highest summit, and more ensuring that its peak is unassailable. Enemies are legion: philistines, critics who defend other faiths, media-folk who promote them, hacks, poetasters and especially other (so-called) poets.

It might be glorious if all poets joined one broad church to preach the gospel of poetry to the world. If infighting ceased, think how much energy could be saved and directed outwards, how much protectiveness and possessiveness could be transformed into generosity. Fine but vulnerable poets would no longer be sapped by paranoia. A ludicrous ideal, of course, because poetry's very process and progress are in part argumentative; it is a dialectical and subversive art. 'Literature,' said Thomas Hardy, 'is the written expression of revolt against all accepted things.' According to Octavio Paz, 'poetry is a food which the bourgeoisie – as a class – has proved incapable of digesting'.

Anyone passionately committed to poetry is disappointed by what does not live up to its name. It's easier to say what it is not than to define, let alone practise it. It's easier to attack than to promote, and simpler to write poets off than to read them; as Sydney Smith is supposed to have remarked, 'I never read a book before reviewing it; it prejudices a man so.' But what is the length and depth of your attention span? How many poets' works can you give a fair and full reading? Editors and critics have their limits too. Before you criticise them, ask yourself whether you read responsibly. It's your job too.

Favouritism and factionalism are not to be wondered at, for humankind cannot bear very much poetry. All you can do is read and write as well as you can.

Any newcomer to the publishing scene is likely to find plenty of fuel for paranoia. It's less painful to feel you've been rejected or badly reviewed because you're misunderstood than because your work is not good enough. 'I can remember wondering as a child if I were a young Macaulay or Ruskin and secretly deciding that I was,' W.N.P. Barbellion confided to his journal. 'My infant mind even was bitter with those who insisted on regarding me as a normal child and not as a prodigy. Since then I have struggled with this canker for many a day, and as success fails to arrive it becomes more gnawing.'

Anger that says, 'I'll show them,' can inspire good work. Bitterness is self-destructive. Eschew it. Of course there are editors who read the work of writers they already know, and of writers who are friends, with greater attention than they'll bring to yours. Rumours of an Oxbridge Mafia are not entirely unfounded. The old poetic school tie is still proudly worn in some quarters. Tribal loyalties are intensely strong, intensely human and intensely destructive. A poet makes friends with other poets in his college because he respects their work. He publishes it when he becomes a publisher. Nothing wrong in that. One of the published friends reviews the poet-publisher's book favourably. Nothing wrong in that; we can be objective in these matters. The reviewer's brother is also a publisher; he brings out the poet-publisher's next book. Nothing wrong in that; we wouldn't like to be seen publishing our own work. We do it all the same, in time, hoping there's nothing wrong in that, and we put forward the name of the reviewer-poet for a literary award. And the second publisher, the reviewer-poet's brother, has a journalist sister-in-law who writes a feature about the latest school of poetry. Nothing wrong in that, except how did a woman get into this scenario? Nothing wrong in that?

And the poets who are not in on this, but went to another university, form a coterie of their own, with their own poetics, their own broadsides against the establishment. And the poets who are not in on any of this, many of the best and the worst, most of us, are loners.

A few of the loners, the women and the black poets are published by the mainstream houses, naturally. It wouldn't be fair otherwise. But Emily Dickinson was almost unpublished in her lifetime:

> 'Tis true – They shut me in the Cold –
> But then – Themselves were warm

Gerard Manley Hopkins too. He wrote of fame as 'a spur very hard to find a substitute for or to do without...What I do regret is the loss of recognition belonging to the work itself...For disappointments and humiliations embitter the heart and make an aching in the very bones.'

There is a comforting myth that great work like theirs will eventually surface despite the publishing establishment's lack of responsibility and perception. How do we know this is true?

There is a comforting myth that if great work is within a writer it will come out, will get written. How do we know this is false? We have Hopkins's testimony that he would have written much more, given encouragement, consistent self-confidence and time: 'It is not possible for me to do anything, unless a sonnet, and that rarely, in poetry with a fagged mind and a continual anxiety.' We know that Marina Tsvetayeva, surviving by drudgery in exile, with children to care for, came up with: 'An astonishing observation: it is precisely for feeling that one needs time, and not for thought... Feeling requires leisure; it cannot survive under fear.' She writes of work, chores, lack of solitude: '...and by 10 at night I am so exhausted – what feeling can there be? Feeling requires *strength*.'

'Poetry is the spontaneous overflow of powerful feelings' runs William Wordsworth's often misquoted definition, 'it takes its origin from emotion recollected in tranquillity.' The T word is good if you can get it. Wordsworth had his struggles, his wounds at critics' hands, but he had colleagues – Coleridge, Southey and all – to affirm his value, his publisher Joseph Cottle, a legacy from Raisley Calvert to enable him to pursue his vocation, his wife Mary to look after him, his sister Dorothy to give him ideas, another legacy, a civil list pension and the status of poet laureate. He died at 80. Hopkins, worn out, succumbed to typhoid at 45. Tsvetayeva hanged herself at 47.

Enough said. There are many demons – publishers, critics, lack of recognition, lack of time, penury, drudgery, sexism, racism, anxiety, depression – which conspire to suppress and effectively silence a poet. There are plenty of real fears, and reasons for paranoia. 'All my life have I not been outside?' wrote Sylvia Plath, 'Ranged against well-meaning foes?'

But let's be positive. 'I do not write for money or fame,' said Marianne Moore. 'One writes because one has a burning desire to objectify what is indispensable to one's happiness to express.' You can but try to find the tranquillity in which to do that, Virginia Woolf's *A Room of One's Own* and all that that implies. Then you face the bogey men that assail you from within and without.

Let's have some good news. I think it's true to say that there have never been so many opportunities for poets to publish. I don't mean that all on the publisher's patio is rosy. But if the main-stream won't let you swim with them, there are many small pools, undercurrents and counter-currents where the water's lovely. I've repeated ad nauseam that it's very difficult to make a splash; you know that, but you've heard that there are tributaries where you can launch yourself modestly, still keeping your ambition intact and your eyes on the ocean.

Let's abandon the metaphor. There are cliques and coteries, there is nepotism and arse-licking, but there is also an appetite for good work by new writers. There is a market for good work by new writers. You don't have to be a friend of the editor. You do have to write bloody well. It's undoubtedly easier if your chair is already drawn up to the fire, but it's quite possible to come in from the cold.

Editors have an enormous responsibility. Some, though human, are exemplary, but you cannot expect to be received by disinterested and open minds. At least you can choose to work in a spirit of openness and generosity yourself; it's too easy to become bitter and literally dispirited. Try not to enrol with a narrow sect; it's comfortable because it shrinks the horizon, the circumference of yourself. Be a loner by all means, but don't become a faction of one; you'd have to develop a proportionately vast demonology with which to flagellate yourself. Look after your daemon, and the demons will look after themselves.

CHAPTER NINE

Pundits and Gurus

'Learn to write well, or not to write at all.' – JOHN DRYDEN

'I have no great faith in the boastful pretensions to intuitive
propriety and unlaboured elegance. The rough material of
Fine Writing is certainly the gift of Genius; but I as firmly
believe that the workmanship is the united effort of Pains,
Attention, and repeated Trial.' – ROBERT BURNS

Demons should be exorcised. Daemons should be exercised. A daemon is one's attendant genius; in this sense, genius is a guiding
spirit, but it also means a natural talent. Here, as elsewhere, the
language of creativity has its head in the ether – to use another old-
fashioned word – and its feet on the ground.

The Muse – whichever of Mnemosyne and Zeus's nine daughters chooses to whisper in your inner ear – is inspiration's source.
Inspiration is also the act of inhaling, breathing in. To muse is to
ponder or meditate; musing sounds like something which poets do
with their noses in the air, but the root of the verb is different from
that of the noun, it comes from the Old Italian or French for *muz-
zle* or *snout* and means to sniff around, to follow a scent; its nose
is not in the air at all, it's down to earth.

The language is confused and confusing. Musing is part of learning, and a genius (guiding spirit) is a teacher. But the Muse speaks
to the chosen, and genius (natural talent) cannot be learned, it's a
gift. We shy away from these words now but we're happy to talk of
the left and right brain: the intellectual/rational versus the emo-
tional/spiritual, male versus female, Ego versus Id, Yang versus Yin.

It seems we need these complementary opposites: half-truths
that might better be called double-truths, paradoxes that must be
held in tension, polarities that flow one into another, contradic-
tions that may be resolved when we've found the words to do it.
But why all this talk of earth and ether, right and left? It becomes
important when we ask the question, where does poetry come from?
Or when we make the useful false distinction between art and craft.
One person says that poetry-writing can't be taught; another says
it can. They're both right.

One says writing is simply hard graft. Another says that work means nothing unless the Muse is invoked, that conscious effort is all in vain if the unconscious mind is shackled or suppressed. Some say glibly that art is 5% inspiration and 95% perspiration. Others, whom Burns would understand, say they can only write when they're inspired, and they make sure they're inspired at 9 o'clock every morning. There's plenty of room for debate because writers experience the process in different ways. Poets, whether or not they admit to dependency upon the Muse, acknowledge how much art they've learned by example and how much craft they've had to master before achieving fluency in their own idiom.

Why is it, then, that so many would-be poets think that poetry writing cannot be taught? They claim that language is their birthright, inspiration is a gift, the words pour out and that's it. Self-expression is not art, though art may be self-expression. Therapy is not poetry, though a lot of poetry is both therapeutic and cathartic. Wilful spontaneity has led many an artist down into the mire.

We all had to learn to speak, to read and to write. A painter has to learn to handle paint and perspective. A composer should do more than hum. A carpenter must understand timber's grain and the structure of snug joints. We value Cézanne, Chopin and Chippendale for more than craftsmanship, but know that craft is essential to the quality of their work.

A blob of paint, a note, a stick of wood mean very little in isolation. Words, a poem's raw material, are already loaded with meaning; everybody uses them; that's why poetry, and the life of a poet, is easy to begin and exceptionally difficult to refine.

Ways of learning

'The lyf so short, the craft so long to lerne,
Thassay so hard, so sharp the conquering.' – CHAUCER

If you're well-educated and have an original mind, huge talent and inspiration, naturally you won't need to take lessons from anybody. Really? Then why did T.S. Eliot submit *The Waste Land* to Ezra Pound's drastic editing; why did he dedicate it to him: '*il miglior fabbro*' – the better craftsman?

Some poets start out with degree courses in Literature – which can inspire or inhibit – but creative writing has mostly been self-taught of necessity. Anyone literate can have a crack at it, after all. Certainly, self-education is a life-long commitment for an artist (see Chapter 12). Why then are there Art Schools, Music Colleges, training courses and apprenticeships for cabinet-makers? Our education system has been ready to train creative and interpretive artists of many kinds, but much more reluctant than that of the United States to nurture novelists and poets.

Things have changed and there are a number of courses on offer with a creative writing component. If you want to study full-time, whether you're a school leaver or a mature student, check the possibilities and entry requirements and get intimate with the work of the poets who are teaching on the courses. Choose your teachers and hope that they choose you.

Few people can take this road. Fewer still have the opportunity to sit at the feet of a poet-guru or to be apprenticed to a master. But for those who want to learn, who want criticism and encouragement, there are several ways of going about it.

Pundits by post

For a fee, the Poetry Society's critical service, The Script, offers comment, criticism and advice on your poems from a tutor, one of a panel of published poets. The School of Poets Critical Service at the Scottish Poetry Library does a similar job; £15 and an s.a.e. buys a response to six poems comprising not more than 200 lines in all. Poetry Ireland's Critical Service charges £30 for ten or so poems, depending on length. The Arts Council of Wales Critical Service (for writers living in Wales) costs £15 for up to 200 lines of poetry (or 3,000 words of prose) and promises a report within ten weeks.

The literature or published media departments of some Regional Arts Boards offer comparable services. Fees vary. Eastern Arts' Write Lines is free and offers a response by professional readers to between 25 and 100 poems. Each region's scheme has its guidelines. Send an s.a.e. to find out exactly what's available in your area and take serious advantage of it. Prepare your manuscript with care, send it as you would to an editor and be ready to take tough though positive advice.

There are private services too. For instance, alongside its publishing activities in Huddersfield – which it calls 'the Poetry Capital of England' – the Poetry Business offers a postal Reading Service as well as Writing Days and Competitions. The National Poetry Foundation provides an appraisal service together with a magazine and information service; it helps its clients towards book publication. Keep an eye on the magazines for new initiatives.

Don't *expect* publishers to give you critical reports on your work. If they do give you some feedback, that's a bonus. They can't spend much time giving critical responses to the thousands of poets they're unable to publish: they have to devote as much of their time as possible to the complex business of editing and producing the books they have been able to accept and publish, often against a background of financial restraints and other difficulties within their publishing house or group. So let them get on with their publishing. If your main need is for critical feedback, look elsewhere.

Face to face

Classes and Workshops run by poets are organised by a variety of bodies: Workers' Educational Association (WEA), university extramural departments, adult education, Regional Arts Boards, libraries, arts centres etc. They vary from single days to weekly evening classes. Each poet has his or her own methods and every group has its own dynamics; many writers have found their first audience, their first critical response, and their first launch into publication from such surroundings. Provision is generous, patchy or sparse, depending on where you live. But if there's no creative writing class nearby, press for one.

Such courses and classes are under pressure from pragmatic, utilitarian forces which see no reason to subsidise education in something so gratuitous, so gloriously useless as poetry. Its contribution to the wealth of our civilisation is unquantifiable. It is, say the ignorant elected guardians of the future, non-vocational. You could try telling them it's your vocation.

Poets-in-the-community or poets-in-residence at libraries, arts centres and colleges offer not only readings and workshops but also devote much of their time to one-to-one surgeries. You are invited to make an appointment to discuss work in depth.

A number of poets – such as Peter Scupham, Anne Cluysenaar, Philip Gross, Helen Dunmore and Jay Ramsay – run workshops or one-to-one apprenticeship schemes of their own.

Living with poets

In 1968 fifteen school children lived as writers with the poets John Moat and John Fairfax at the Beaford Centre in Devon. The energy that was released there, in living and writing together, was so vital and productive that the poets knew they'd created a pattern that had to be followed. The Arvon Foundation was born. It has one centre at Totleigh Barton in Devon, one at Lumb Bank in Yorkshire, and another at Moniack Mhor in Inverness-shire.

It is impossible to sum up what the Arvon experience has given to students and tutors. It has changed many lives. For five days of extraordinary intensity two established writers and up to sixteen students live and work, walk and write together. A guest writer gives a mid-week reading. Each course is different; tutors respond to the variety of needs they find. Each writer rubs up against a range of sensibilities and sees a new horizon of possibilities. Some develop dramatically within the week; others reap the benefit later when the experience has sunk in. I've witnessed wonderful growth, both painful and joyful, and triumphant work during weeks at Lumb and Totleigh.

If you're short of cash there are bursaries administered by the Arvon Foundation as well as grants towards the fees offered by some RABs. Ask for a bursary application form when you send an s.a.e. for details of the year's courses. But don't apply for financial help, as one of my students did, and then arrive at the course in expensive clothes and a white Mercedes.

Other centres, like Tŷ Newydd, the Taliesin Trust's centre in Gwynedd, have deliberately followed the Arvon pattern, as has The Poet's House set up by James and Janice Fitzpatrick Simmons in Northern Ireland. Fen Farm in East Anglia runs similar courses with one tutor. And it's possible now to fly off to France or Spain for writing weeks in the sun. The essence of the best courses is simple: a community of concentration, openness, ambition and humility; apprentices learning from each other and from master craftsmen.

Ted Hughes contributed a foreword to *The Way to Write* by John Fairfax and John Moat. In it he confesses how negative his first reaction to the Arvon idea had been. He examines his prejudices, that are shared by many who cannot believe that such a simple notion can work. He had seen literary apprenticeship in action: Anne Sexton learning from Robert Lowell who had, in turn, served his time under Allen Tate and John Crowe Ransom; but that was in America. Would such a thing agree with the English temperament? Despite his misgivings he was the guest reader on the first Arvon course. He saw that what had happened that week was more remarkable than anything he'd previously witnessed. He was converted.

Submitting to teachers is sobering and inspiring. It gives you permission to write. It allows you to possess your talent, and to refine your craft. It puts you in a real context, in the world of living literature. It puts those myths, half-truths and neuroses about creativity in their place. And you in yours.

See Listings, pages 104 & 105.

CHAPTER TEN

Nice Little Earners

'...Sentry over old songs and nothing special,
Exiled to not-explaining, expected to do well,
Sentenced to endless hospitality of the innocent,
Trying not to bite, to be human...'
FROM *In Residence* by U.A. FANTHORPE

'There is something intrinsically sordid in adopting poetry
as a profession...' – CHARLES OSBORNE

There are jobs poets can do which are easier than writing poetry. Like being an opera critic, a lavatory attendant, an accountant or Literature Director of the Arts Council. There are also jobs poets can do, as poets, which are easier than writing poetry. Like editing magazines, giving readings, making broadcasts, leading workshops and creative writing seminars, being a poet-in-school, university, library, arts centre, prison or anywhere else a poet can take up short- or long-term residence.

You'll have got an idea of the range of rôles a poet can play from earlier chapters. You have to establish a local or national reputation before you can tout for jobs. Many are only possible if you are a freelance writer or can get leave from work. You also have to be sure that spin-off jobs are what you really want to do; they can drain you of the creative energy you need for your poetry; you may not be a good performer or teacher however brilliant your writing is.

Poets find it easy to earn a lot more from such jobs than from publishing their work, but that's not saying much. Mostly the jobs are not well paid. They are nice *little* earners. Some writers have to work so hard at them to make a living and spend so many hours travelling the country, staying in spare rooms or lodgings or hotels, that too little time is left for writing. It's probably best to remain an amateur (in the best sense) poet but, when a related job possibility comes your way, to approach applying for and performing it with all the professionalism you can muster.

Readings

If you're good, word spreads. Invitations come, and in each new situation you have a chance to sell your books. In chapter four I gave an example of how not to do a reading. If you're asked to perform, agree with the organiser, in advance and in writing, exactly how the event will be shaped. Agree a fee that does not undercut the going rate (£100 plus). Make sure that travelling expenses will be paid on top of the fee, and that you will be met if need be. Make sure the organiser knows that you expect to be given your cheque after the reading, if payment is being made by the organiser or organisation hosting the reading; you should only have to wait to receive your cheque in the post afterwards if it is being paid by a reputable third party, such as a Regional Arts Board, local authority or libraries department. There are pitfalls in giving readings: having to chase organisers for cheques; paying out for train fares and not being reimbursed for some time, which can make things difficult if you're doing a lot of readings; wasting time dealing with arts, college or local authority bureaucracies; and worst of all, giving a reading at a one-off festival whose administration apparently self-destructs on the last day. Do not agree to read for a students' union or a college or university literary society unless they promise in writing to give you your cheque on the day of the reading: students are often inexperienced in the business side of running events, and student organisations are notorious for not paying poets and for delaying payments. A meal should be provided; be clear about any dietary requirements; your stomach/nerves may prefer food before or after your performance. Check what overnight accommodation you will get; a spare room in the organiser's house may be more to your taste than an hotel room, but sweet repose in a blanket on a draughty floor or snug in a poetry groupie's bed may or may not be your idea of fun.

Plan your reading. Think about your links. Note anything that you *must* say before you read a poem – the meaning of a dialect word it contains for example. Script the whole thing if you need to, but make it sound ad lib. Pause after each poem to let it sink in. Don't waffle abstractedly while you shuffle through reams of paper for the next one. I always make a list of what I'm going to read, with page numbers against the poems in books, and unpublished poems in order in a folder. If there's going to be an interval, structure your programme so that two halves make sense. If you're on with other poets, you can plan to read complementary or contrasting work. Time your part of the reading, and then cut back some of your programme; it always takes longer live.

That's the rehearsal. Before the real thing, talk to any other writers who are taking part, agree upon the length of each person's contribution and stick to it. Be sure that the MC knows how to introduce you and points out the stack of books you're willing to sign. You'll sell more copies if you read from a book, if you have one, rather than a typescript. Breathe well. Project your voice. As you gain confidence it will be easier to improvise in front of an audience, to put poems in because they seem appropriate, and to take them out because your close watch on the clock – you did notice when you began didn't you? – tells you you're overrunning. You'll learn how your nerves react and what the adrenalin's doing. You may not think of yourself as a performance poet, rather a sober reader of living literature, but this is showbiz all the same. Break a leg!

Workshops and Surgeries

Once you've done a few readings, you may get asked to run poetry workshops. The success of readings, broadcasts and appearances at literary festivals depends upon the vitality of your work and your presentation of it. Teaching in any form requires other virtues: enthusiasm for your subject, confidence in your command of it, an instinct for group dynamics, empathy with individuals and, not least, patience.

Think back to what I said about editors. When student poets present work to you, you'll feel all the editorial frustrations, but face to face, en masse or, worse, one to one. It's essential that you like people, that you have faith in the process of poetry, whatever the end-product is like. Should you praise over-fulsomely for encour-agement's sake? Do you tear bad work to shreds? Do you say, I'm sorry, I can't help you? Do you search for *something* you can praise? You need both tact and honesty. You're expected to be marriage guidance counsellor, Citizens' Advice Bureau, psychiatrist, priest, Samaritan and, sometimes, poet. You have to decide which rôles you're prepared to play. You must switch rapidly from one person's psychic universe to another's. You have to be flexible and consis-tent. You live for the moments when, out of the blue, an authentic voice strikes your ear: real promise, unpretentious achievement, poetry.

It's hard to separate lives and works, biography and craft. You'll wish your life was longer, their art shorter. After hours of writers' surgeries you'd swear that dentists and ear-nose-and-throat spec-ialists were hardly more skilled than you in the topography of the human mouth. Dentists have more dignity; ENT specialists don't have to share the credit with their patients; some of the time solicitors have more fun commissioning oaths.

You see, I don't want you to be under any romantic delusions about these spin-off jobs. They're exhausting, frustrating but often stimulating too. On balance I find the work very rewarding and full of unpredictable enjoyment.

Appearance and Reality

Librarians, teachers and others who host residencies don't always know how to deal with a poet. A live one, that is. Sometimes you get the reverence reserved for god. Sometimes you're a little shit who thinks he's Tennyson. Often you're an ethereal in-between creature whose concern is Art, whose food is ambrosia and who needs nowhere to lay his head.

As with readings make sure the contract is very specific about working and, where appropriate, living conditions. I once took up a residency funded jointly by the Arts Council and a nameless college. The interviews had been exacting, optimism was in the air. Everyone was pleasant, respectful and excited about the post's potential. I was to be given a room in the college as my working base, and a flat to live in. The flat turned out to be draughty high-ceilinged kitchen quarters at one end of a large house ten miles from the college. Both furniture and cooking facilities were makeshift. It was autumn term. I could hardly believe how damp and icy it was. With the coal fire blazing I could just nudge the temperature to within ten degrees of the acceptable minimum for the prevention of hypothermia.

My college office was a store room threaded through with hot-water pipes; there were no windows. It was stale, stifling. The staff were great. The students were willing. The work was good, though hard to slot into an intractable timetable. Some exciting things happened. But, shunting between airless heat and damp winter cold, I became ill. Naturally, poets as a species are adapted to life in garrets. But not to work in sweat-shops at the same time. Many writers have horror stories. Be warned. Now it's possible to be a Writer-in-Residence on the Internet. Cyberspace may sound inhospitable but at least you can control the draughts.

Soliciting work

A good moment to start looking for readings is when your first pamphlet or book comes out. It provides the occasion for such a launch. Given plenty of notice your regional literature officer or local authority arts development officer may be able to help by putting you in touch with organisers. More information about these and about national agencies is given in the next chapter. Secure yourself an entry in the Writers' Directory issued by your RAB or its equivalent, and in listings kept by national bodies – Arts Councils, Poetry Society etc – for use by those who are looking for poets to give readings or to work in education.

When you are ready to tackle a poet-in-schools job or a residency, keep an eye on the press and literary newsletters, and contact any artists' organisations in your area such as the Artists' Agency in Sunderland (they arrange a wide variety of residencies in schools, factories, libraries and other places). Depending on the sort of job you feel suited to, be sure that relevant employers are aware of your presence – arts officers, English advisors, chief librarians etc. Make applications. Don't be shy, but don't hype yourself beyond credulity.

Some writers circulate a sheet or leaflet which is part CV, part "blurb". If, for instance, it is aimed at schools it will contain details of relevant qualifications and/or experience, your publications, perhaps review quotes and, most important, a run-down on what you offer: readings, talks, poetry workshops, oracy and writing projects. It will indicate your approach and specify the size and age-range of groups you like to work with; it will set out suggestions to teachers for preparatory and follow-up work. It will state your fee and explain how to apply for grant aid and to whom. It will be aimed at your target, clearly and persuasively. Be concise, businesslike, inspiring.

You can suggest to local papers and magazines that you contribute a lively poetry column. You can put up the idea for a poetry programme to your local radio station. You know your patch; see where you can start, see how far you can go. Tact, persuasiveness and imaginative flair can take you a long way.

Sordid Maud

'I spent so much of my life teaching and lecturing and reading
...that I had not time or energy to write the things that I have
really begun. I have 3 unfinished books which were the main
objects of my life. I am 85 years old...' – KATHERINE ANNE PORTER

A writer's is a tough life. There is something intrinsically difficult about adopting poetry as a profession: it's hard making a living. But there's nothing intrinsically sordid about it. Charles Osborne, whom I quote at the beginning of this chapter, had a long reign as Literature Director at the Arts Council in London. That's partly why public patronage for writers in England still lags behind that of Scotland, Wales and Ireland. His attitudes are no longer current at the ACGB, but there are still élitists about who look only to the great dead, and don't realise that the great dead often died sooner rather than later for lack of money, for want of unencumbered time in which to pursue their vocation.

Very few poets have earned a good living. After Maud was published in 1855, Tennyson earned more than £2000 a year from writing. (A sordid but fortunately rare exception!) What poet earns the equivalent today? There are some cultures where the profession of poetry is revered, and a few where poets are revered and read and paid. Still, we can do all we can to make poetry valued here and, when we're not doing other jobs poets can do, we can return to the hardest task, writing the poems that will pulse in the wordstream of the twenty-first century.

CHAPTER ELEVEN

Allies

'We aim to speak up for poetry and poets and to introduce the public at large to the strength and diversity of our poetry heritage and to the important work going on today.' – POETRY SOCIETY

'The starting point of literature lies in the human imagination and spirit...We aim to support new writing as well as help people gain access to books...' – ARTS COUNCIL OF GREAT BRITAIN

In preceding chapters I've said quite a lot about what the Arts Councils, Regional Arts Boards and Associations, Poetry Libraries and other agencies can do. Arts officers and animateurs are enablers, advisors, allies. They cannot be muses. They won't help you to write your poems. They're not publishers. They won't give grants towards self-publication, or any kind of grant at the drop of a hat. Nor will they buy you a word-processor.

Although they do try to give individuals support and advice, bear in mind that time and resources don't allow literature officers to act as Citizens' Advice Bureaux, mentors, counsellors or literary agents. They deal with hundreds of enquiries by phone and post in any week, as well as getting on with development work and lobbying for more money for literature from their own boards, local authorities, government and from sponsors. Increasingly arts bodies are development agencies that work in partnership with groups and organisations, rather than on a one-to-one basis with individual writers.

So what use are they? Because policies shift in response to perceived needs and constraints (and because the English Regional Arts Associations were reorganised as Boards, with some boundary changes, in 1991) it is impossible to summarise exactly what is offered by arts bodies at any one time. Each region has its own priorities and therefore different criteria for its use of public money. The relationship between the Arts Councils and subsidiary agencies differs sometimes substantially and often subtly as between Ireland, Northern Ireland, Scotland, Wales and England.

But they are very useful. Through them every writer has access to information about what's going on, to their magazines and/or newsletters, to critical services, writers' directories, to writers in education schemes, readings and tours, fellowships, residencies and placements. Many magazines receive grant-aid; some book publishers have revenue grants and others are awarded money for particular titles. There are grants towards courses for new publishers, small press and magazine editors, literature promoters and community workers. Some are given to encourage cultural diversity and are awarded specifically to people of African, Caribbean or Asian origin. Bursaries and grants to enable individuals to buy time to write, translate, travel or research are administered by Arts Councils and a few regional bodies. Here, as always, it's chickens, eggs and Catch-22: the more established you are, the more likely you are to get them.

Even if you're on the starting line I strongly advise you to get in touch with your literature officer or development worker (see *Listings*). Ring first and check the name and job title – these things change – then write, simply asking what services are on offer to poets in your area. Many produce excellent writer's information packs. They will tell you about local magazines, publishers, writers' groups, writers in residence, and about development officers or animateurs employed by local authorities. Literature officers respond to initiatives too: if you have some track record and a brilliant idea for a project, especially if it's in line with current policy, it's well worth making the effort to sell it to a grant-giving body.

'Literature Officer', and its variants, can sound comic or sinister depending on your mood. However bureaucratic the hoops through which they and you must jump, they do have human faces. Approach them as people committed to writing. Don't be diffident or defensive. You are unique and your talent is precious, but you don't have to prove yourself in every communication. Be human too and you won't blow it. They deal with people like you every day. They may not be muses or great critics but their advice is worth listening to. One complained, 'Unfortunately, enquirers are often much more interested in publishing their work than in improving it.' Another said, 'Misconceptions do take up a lot of time. We also (only occasionally, I am glad to say) come in for some abuse. One charming gentleman told us that we would not know a poem from the end of a fucking elephant.'

Societies

It's hard to explain the difference, but the Poetry Society might help. The Poetry Society is based in London's Covent Garden It publishes *Poetry Review* and a members' newsletter, *Poetry News*; it offers a Critical Service, The Script, and administers both the

National Poetry Competition and the European Poetry Translation Prize. It contributes to national promotions such as National Poetry Day and Poetry for Christmas. Its educational projects include the administration of the free W.H. Smith Poets in Schools Scheme and the publication of *BP Teachers' Poetry Resources Files*, Poetry Posters (with teachers' notes) and a *Young Poetry Pack*. Its Lottery-funded Poetry Café is available for book launches and literary events. Seminars and workshops are run in its Reading Room, which offers information on all aspects of poetry and writing. At stations in the Poetry Café, or anywhere in the world, you can browse the Society's news, information and inspiration service at its Internet site, *The Poetry Map*, which can be accessed at http://www.bbcnc.org.uk/online/poetry.

The Irish poetry society is Poetry Ireland in Dublin; it runs the Austin Clarke Library, publishes *Poetry Ireland Review* and a bi-monthly newsletter; it has links with eighty writers' groups and with arts centres in thirty-two counties. Poetry Ireland organises countrywide readings by poets from Ireland and abroad; its Intro-duction Readings give a platform to three new poets at a time. Poetry competition winners are published in broadsheet and book form. In collaboration with Trinity College, Dublin, Poetry Ireland publish an annual Trinity Workshop Poets anthology. Its Critical Service is open to writers in English and Irish. Poetry Ireland Choice is a bookclub which selects four new collections of Irish poetry each year, three in English and one in the Irish language.

The Welsh Academy is the English Language Section of Yr Academi Gymreig in Cardiff; it promotes literature in Wales and has much to offer poets. There are three tiers of membership, with associate membership open to all who wish to receive the Academy's bulletin, BWA, and regular mailings with details of activities, com-petitions, writing courses etc. It publishes *The New Welsh Review* and organises the annual Cardiff Literature Festival and its Inter-national Poetry Competition; it promotes readings, workshops and an annual conference; it administers the Young Writers' Competition and the John Tripp Award.

Take these organisations, add to them the Poetry Libraries based in Edinburgh, Dublin, Morpeth and London (with the Voice Box and the South Bank Literature Department), mix in the festivals, poetry societies and writers' groups all over Britain and Ireland, and you have a recipe for the nourishment of poets and their public.

Other Allies

If we want them there are allies. When we're not in love with our solitariness, we need some semblance of solidarity. We need to unite our individual, and individualistic, voices to say and demand things for the benefit of writers in general.

The Society of Authors is an independent trade union; the Writers' Guild of Great Britain is a trade union affiliated to the TUC. The first has its roots in the world of books, the second in the media, but both represent all kinds of writers and do fine work on our behalf, arguing with publishers for a Minimum Terms Book Agreement, negotiating with the media for minimum rates, terms and conditions, protecting copyright, campaigning for PLR (Public Lending Right) and its maintenance, etc.

They produce informative publications for members and give help and advice on fees, contracts, agents, publishers, broadcasting companies, legal problems and so on. The Society of Authors administers a number of awards. Both offer many other benefits and if you have had a full-length work published or broadcast, or a contract for one, you are eligible for membership. I believe that professional writers are obliged to support one or other of these organisations that work hard to make life easier for their members and others alike.

What about agents? There's a cliché that an agent is as hard to get as a publisher. It's true. It's also true that, almost without exception, agents will only handle a poet's work if the poet is also a novelist, biographer, playwright, travel writer or broadcaster, in other words if there's some money to be made. Some writers who are good at business would rather keep the 10% and negotiate contracts themselves. I prefer to talk writing rather than money with publishers and producers; for me the money is well spent. If you write things other than poetry I suggest you trawl the extremely useful *Writers' and Artists' Yearbook*, or ask advice from published writers, or the writers' unions, on which agency to approach.

So, there are plenty of allies for poets and for writers in general. From the Arts Councils down the network is extensive, if patchy. It duplicates and omits. It's effective and wasteful. It's idealistic and pragmatic. It's full of energy and inertia. It favours tradition and the flavour of the month. But it's there and you can make connections that will help. As an apprentice writer, discover what's on offer that will help you become a better writer. When you're good make sure the network knows it, but don't sell yourself as the greatest thing since H.D. until you've a few notches on your pencil.

See Listings, pages 100–02.

CHAPTER TWELVE

Toolkits and Workboxes

'Literature is no one's private ground; literature is common ground. Let us trespass freely and fearlessly and find our own way for ourselves.' – VIRGINIA WOOLF

Given all that I've said about penury, it's fortunate that poetry is not a capital intensive occupation. What freedom, to be able to work almost anytime, anywhere, at least in theory. You need only invest in pencil and paper to begin with. Then a typewriter or a word-processor. Envelopes, stamps, international reply coupons. What more do you want?

Fetishes

Even with such limited raw materials it's possible to develop powerful fetishes about them. One poet cannot write unless she has a 2B lead pencil, frequently sharpened, and a particular brand of black-covered hardback notebook with feint-ruled lines 8mm apart and no margin. Another is utterly impotent when he's parted from his battered portable typewriter. A third is addicted to his desk where paper, pens, pencils and reference books must be precisely disposed like a stage set for the Muse. A fourth is powerless off the screen; the word-processor is her crystal ball in which flickers the green fire of creativity.

It's reasonable to have preferences. The movement, at a comfortable pressure, of a pencil over the right grade of paper has a physicality which satisfyingly incarnates the inner world. I like it, especially for my first drafts, but I also like the flexibility of words on screen: how, without crossings out, cramped insertions or scrawled arrows, changes can be made in a text almost as fast as I think them. I don't find the technology alienating; it makes the mind and the page (screen) more intimate and gives their relationship fluidity. At the draft stage I feel that a typewriter is unwieldy, though other writers disagree.

My old typewriter's in the attic. I have a small loose-leaf notebook for my pocket, A4 hardback notebooks for drafts, and a word-processor on my desk. Those are my preferences, though in practice I'll scribble on the back of anything with anything that writes if I'm caught short without the notebook and pen which in theory I carry everywhere like real writers are supposed to do.

Preferences are fine. Fetishes can back-fire. So often we build up superstitious rituals, like actors and athletes, which we become bound to enact before the Muse can speak, before we can make contact with our genius, before the unconscious can surface, before we can side-step the block that waits to ambush us at every turn. Our writing tools can be part of this, along with cups of coffee or camomile tea, background music or utter silence, cigarettes or pep pills...These habits are so much bullshit. I know, I've some of my own. Some aren't. There are productive habits which you will discover or be taught. All I'm saying here is don't be inhibited by rituals. Don't turn gear which should free you into a constraint. If too much has to be just so before you can write a word, you can guarantee you won't write very often. The chiming of the liberty bell comes to sound like the jangling of chains.

Beware of building too much mythology around your own creative process. You can delve into it and be practical about it without denting your genius or defusing your talent, unless you've shrouded it with mystique. Mystique is very vulnerable. It's good for a poet to eavesdrop on other poets' processes, to take advice and make discoveries through their experience. It's useful to scrutinise your own sacred cows, your own bullshit in the light of theirs, and of their wisdom.

The Poet's Bookshelf
What more do you want then? Books. Books are tools of the trade too. A writer's necessary obsession with them can be very costly but they must be bought or borrowed and read hungrily.

Books about poetry, books about writing, books about words: these should sit, alongside all the books of poetry, on a poet's shelves. Why waste years and exhaust your brain, learning or failing to learn from mistakes out of misbegotten pride in poetic self-sufficiency, when so many writers have put their hard-learned lessons on record? When Hugh Kingsmill was asked what he'd do if he had his life over again, he considered the question carefully before responding, 'I should use fewer commas and more semi-colons.' Not as flippant as it sounds. Here are some titles comprising a self-education course which affords both inspiration and information: incitement to invention, plus workshop manuals, spanners and feeler-gauges.

Becoming a Writer by Dorothea Brande is a classic which challenges the idea that genius cannot be taught. It enables any writer to demystify the writing process, without being reductive, and provides techniques and liberating disciplines by means of which we can get in touch with 'the writer's magic'. It is not primarily aimed at poets, but is indispensable for all that.

The Way to Write by John Fairfax and John Moat is a practical and life-enhancing book, full of insight and humour, which takes you from the blank page to the publisher's doorstep. Again it is for writers in general, but both authors are poets and its warnings and exhortations are pertinent.

The Way to Write Poetry by Michael Baldwin gets to the heart of things; it is practical and poetical in style; its exercises and exposition of forms are demanding and generous; it hints and nudges but leaves you free to get on with your own work in your own way, though less naively and more resourcefully than before.

Writing Poems by Peter Sansom, Bloodaxe's second Poetry Handbook, is down-to-earth and inspirational. Sansom writes about conviction and technique. He demonstrates how to write authentically and how to nurture your own creative process and self-critical faculty: how to say genuinely what you genuinely mean to say.

What to do with your poems by Evangeline Paterson tells you how to edit your own work, submit it for publication and present it at readings. Written by an experienced magazine editor, it is full of useful hints and inside information.

Berthing: A Poetry Workbook by Gillian Allnutt, with an accompanying cassette, is one of a series of courses on women's literature and history produced by the National Extension College/Virago. It aims to break down barriers that academicism, bad education, racism and sexism have erected; it encourages its readers to find their way in to poetry, to be nourished by it and to write it, so that it becomes more central to life and culture.

The Poet's Handbook by Judson Jerome is a comprehensive if conservative exposition of, and guide to, metrical writing; it's sceptical about too much modernism, but excellent as a reference work on the art and mechanics of verse and free verse, and on the business of being a working poet.

The Princeton Encyclopedia of Poetry and Poetics edited by Alex Preminger is a huge (992 pages) compendium with detailed entries or articles on virtually everything you'll ever want to know about poetry's history, types (from many different cultures), movements, prosody and critical terminology.

Metre, Rhyme and Free Verse by G.S. Fraser is a fine, useful book which will enlarge your appreciation of poetry, and enhance your technical competence and confidence.

How Poetry Works: the elements of English poetry by Philip Davies Roberts could have been called 'How poetry sounds'; an interesting historical and critical survey, illustrated by an anthology.

Twentieth-Century Poetry: Critical Essays and Documents, edited by Graham Martin and P.N. Furbank. Produced to accompany an Open University course this anthology (now out of print) of critical writings gathers together many of the classic modern critical texts, including essays on poetry by Yeats, Eliot, Auden, Empson, Pound and Leavis.

Modern Poets on Modern Poetry edited by James Scully is a brilliant anthology of poets' writings which illuminate and justify their own matter and methods; they stir and jar you into new ways of looking at the variety of poetic enterprise. This book will lead you on to books by its contributors, many of which I would recommend. You'll have to borrow it because it's out of print. Or buy:

Poets at Work: The Paris Review Interviews by George Plimpton which allows you to eavesdrop on sixteen poets including Ezra Pound, T.S. Eliot, Marianne Moore, William Carlos Williams, W.H. Auden, Robert Lowell, Anne Sexton, Allen Ginsberg and John Ashbery.

Silences by Tillie Olsen is a moving testament to all that blocks creativity and silences writers. It's a requiem for work that has never been born, but it is also an inspiring account of how authors – many of them women or black writers – have at great cost triumphed over class, sexual and racial prejudice, social or political circumstance, depression, critical assault and lack of patronage to persist in doing at least some of the work of which they were capable. It should be compulsory reading for every Arts Minister, Literature Officer and publisher.

The Penguin Rhyming Dictionary edited by Rosalind Fergusson comes into the category of reference works – several more follow that some purists say a true poet should not need. This is snobbish superstition; don't turn your nose up at tools which are available at least as last resorts. This one is the best available to the (relatively) standard English ear.

The Poet's Manual and Rhyming Dictionary by Frances Stillman has a good introduction on poetics genres – epic, narrative, lyric, light, etc – and sections on rhythm and metre, rhyme, traditional forms, free verse, modernist methods, content and style; it's a little po-faced but still very useful.

Roget's Thesaurus is another book you shouldn't need, but often do. It's the poet's business to find the exact word, the one that sounds right, to find an Anglo-Saxon alternative for the Latinate word in your head, or to avoid unproductive repetition by the skilful use of synonyms. A thesaurus helps and should not be despised.

Fowler's Modern English Usage can clear up troublesome questions of grammar, syntax and style. If you have difficulty writing clear prose, you'll certainly need help with poetry.

The Oxford Guide to the English Language includes Dr E.S.C. Weiner's *Oxford Guide to English Usage* and is a useful handbook. It gives guidance on word formations, points of grammar, syntax, punctuation and pronunciation; it explains frequently misused or confused words and warns against clichés and modish and inflated diction. Good and bad usage is illustrated by quotations from contemporary and recent writers' work. These sections are followed by a *c.*30,000-word dictionary.

A good dictionary is an essential tool. I use the compact edition of the *Oxford English Dictionary*, magnifying glass and all, because I like etymology and illustrative quotations *in extenso*. To complement this you need an up-to-date shorter dictionary – browse and choose one that suits you – that includes current usage, including new coinings and imports. You may find that the most recent Concise or Shorter Oxford English Dictionary or their Chambers or Collins counterparts – are sufficient for your needs. But don't stint yourself, you're buying a goldmine. Publishers tend to adopt either Oxford or Chambers as their "house" dictionaries and edit all their books to conform with them.

How to Publish your Poetry by Peter Finch, an experienced publisher/editor as well as poet, is the best guide to getting your work into print, and especially good as an introduction to the mechanics of self-publishing.

This list could be extended indefinitely – more reference books are included in *Listings* – and each year sees new titles to warp your shelves a little more. Don't leave them on the shelf, unless you believe that by rubbing your elbow along their spines you can absorb their virtue, but make a contract with yourself to use them purposefully – to stimulate and educate yourself, to demystify and deepen your creative processes and to solve everyday poetic problems. You can't do all that by instinct, and the Muse only helps those that help themselves. Believe it.

See Listings, page 111.

CHAPTER THIRTEEN

The Muse is not amused

'Nothing so difficult as a beginning
In poesy, unless perhaps the end.' – BYRON

'If I could concisely explain I myself or poems or my poems or
writing them, I should not try to write them.' – GEOFFREY GRIGSON

So, the Muse helps those that help themselves, and is not amused
by those who have the nerve to call themselves poets but are unwilling to read and learn. There are many big, and sometimes
powerful, fish thrashing the water in small ponds, but the ocean
of poetry is broad and deep. This book invites you to dive in and
train yourself to swim strongly. I have tried to simplify and summarise but, having dipped your toe in the water, you may well be
chilled by the enormity of the world in which you want to immerse
yourself. Some popularisers strive to make poetry chatty and comfortable. It is not a heated swimming pool. Its glory is that it can
comprehend the dimensions of human experience. That is what is
so attractive about it, and challenging to those who allow themselves to be naked, vulnerable, courageous. 'I think the poet has one
skin too few,' says Sylvia Kantaris, 'and that it *hurts*.' The rest can
play poems in the rock-pools or build word-castles on the beach.

In this book I have blithely used the word "poet" to mean one
who writes poems. It's a big title to take on. Perhaps everybody
who writes them could *become* a poet; very few do. So many people
write self-indulgently without the benefit of reading what poets
have written. Fine poets are unsupported by readers. Editor after
editor confirms this view: would-be poets would do better to take
time out and read before thinking that they can write. Perhaps
they think they can publish because the critical apparatus has fall-
en apart; if poetry's roulette, why not?

'Muse? Um...that's it: Museum, that's where *she* should go!' The
old-fashioned language of creativity is full of mythology in at least
two of its senses: archetypal tales that define us and mistaken bel-
iefs that block us. In the academy engagement with poetry has been
less of a priority than literary theory. The muse has been deconstructed, the author is dead, language precedes meaning, a text is
a text is a text. On the other hand, literary journalists are too often

concerned with the cult of the author, with lauding the like-minded few and damning or, worse, ignoring the rest.

There are stimulating, committed critics at work – Edna Longley and Terry Eagleton for example – whose books and magazine articles are enlightening explorations that don't set your teeth on edge with the grinding of axes. Poets tend to be pessimistic: when *Agenda* asked for comments on contemporary British poetry, George Barker said that during the years he'd been looking for it he'd 'only glimpsed it once and I think it was called a Tony Harrison'. But Harrison is dedicated to craft in the traditional sense and is attacked for his formalism by poets who look to, say, Geoffrey Hill, or to Lee Harwood. Harrison demonstrates that form can contain a strong, utterly contemporary voice, while postmodernists are quite capable of a genteel and etiolated aestheticism. Paradoxes abound. You must read the poems, read the criticism and find your own idiom, one which is true for you.

There is optimism too. Despite the white male London hegemony, real and imagined, women's voices are better heard now, radically different poetries are recognised within Britain and Ireland, neglected poets are being rediscovered, and excellent translations – Bobrowski, Machado, Tranströmer, Jaccottet and many more – nourish us. Those who sit on their insular laurels look increasingly foolish. Much, though not all, of the vital poetry around is published by smaller presses far from the centre, while the commercial publishers too often tie themselves to hyped fads and mainstream fashions. What else should we expect? Fine poets are individualistic, living on the fringes, metaphorical and geographical, of the literary scene.

If you still feel on the outside, remember that most poets do. Find your allies. Use the available resources. Avoid careerism, but behave with professionalism. Don't go for a meteoric rise. Eschew premature knowingness. Slow down and be grateful for each poem. Be ambitious and humble. Be full of the work, not full of yourself. Miroslav Holub, a distinguished immunologist and a poet, smiled and said, 'I don't know why people come to listen to my poems, they're crazy.' John Ashbery wrote of poetry, 'I think people confuse it with the Salvation Army.' But when you can smell the smoke don't fiddle with words. There are important things to say, and important poems shrug off trends, they always have done. Jaroslav Seifert said, 'If an ordinary person is silent about the truth, it may be a tactical manoeuvre. If a writer is silent, he is lying.' And there is inspiration within you, without you. Take a deep breath and write.

CHAPTER FOURTEEN

Landmarks

'The messages of great poems to each man and woman are,
Come to us on equal terms, only then can you understand us.'
— WALT WHITMAN

'Contemporary acclaim has little to do with poetry. What a
poet wants to do is to give life to a few words, words that will
carry over the years, and speak directly to a reader or hearer
in the inner voice of the mind. It's almost impossible. Even
great poets do it rarely.' — PETER DALE

Chapter Two was a sketch map of twentieth-century poetry. In this
chapter I will point out some landmarks. It is a reader's guide, a
selective listing of important poetry collections, influential anthologies and significant individual poems.

Key collections

Hundreds of poets have published hundreds of poetry collections
since the War. Most poets established their reputations with certain individual collections; sometimes one is particularly important, sometimes several. There isn't room here to give a full listing
of individual collections by all the major poets. Once poets are established they will usually publish a *Selected* or *Collected Poems*, and
by that stage those books are the best ones to read, but they are not
included here, except where the poet's work was not widely recognised until a *Selected* or *Collected* was published. The following
listing of key collections published each year forms an illuminating
chronicle of recent literary history. More books and more different
kinds of poets were published from the 1960s onwards, and this is
reflected in the listing, which is mainly of British and Irish writers,
although some American poets are also included where their collections have been influential in Britain. As well as major collections by major writers, significant début volumes are included, as
well as books which enjoyed notoriety or popularity in a particular
year. Countries in brackets (USA, etc) are the place of first publication, and not always the author's country of origin. Books are
listed in the year of publication in Britain. *An asterisk denotes
posthumous publication.

1939: T.S. Eliot: *Old Possum's Book of Practical Cats*; Geoffrey Grigson: *Several Observations*; Louis MacNeice: *Autumn Journal*; Stephen Spender: *The Still Centre*; W.B. Yeats: *Last Poems.**

1940: W.H. Auden: *Another Time*; John Betjeman: *Old Lights for New Chancels*; William Empson: *The Gathering Storm*.

1941: W.H. Auden: *New Year Letter*; W.R. Rodgers: *Awake! and Other Poems*; Vernon Watkins: *The Ballad of the Mari Lwyd*.

1942: Roy Fuller: *The Middle of a War*; Patrick Kavanagh: *The Great Hunger*; Stephen Spender: *Ruins and Visions*.

1943: Norman MacCaig: *Far Cry*; David Gascoyne: *Poems 1937-1942*; Kathleen Raine: *Stone and Flower*; Dylan Thomas: *New Poems*.

1944: W.H. Auden: *For the Time Being*; T.S. Eliot: *Four Quartets*; Roy Fuller: *A Lost Season*; Alun Lewis: *Ha! Ha! among the Trumpets.**

1945: John Betjeman: *New Bats in Old Belfries*; Walter de la Mare: *The Burning-Glass*; Randall Jarrell: *Little Friend, Little Friend* (USA); Philip Larkin: *The North Ship* (new edition 1966).

1946: Elizabeth Bishop: *North and South* (USA); Roy Campbell: *Talking Bronco*; Richard Church: *The Lamp*; Walter de la Mare: *The Traveller*; Robert Graves: *Poems 1938-1945*; Dylan Thomas: *Deaths and Entrances*.

1947: Frances Bellerby: *Plash Mill*; Patrick Kavanagh: *A Soul for Sale*; Stephen Spender: *Poems of Dedication*.

1948: W.H. Auden: *The Age of Anxiety*; Hamish Henderson: *Elegies for the Dead in Cyrenaica*; Randall Jarrell: *Losses* (USA).

1949: Frances Bellerby: *The Brightening Cloud*; Roy Fuller: *Epitaphs and Occasions*; Edwin Muir: *The Labyrinth*; Ezra Pound: *The Pisan Cantos* (USA); Theodore Roethke: *The Lost Son* (USA 1948).

1950: Robert Lowell: *Poems 1938-1949* (USA).

1951: Keith Douglas: *Collected Poems;** Jack Clemo: *The Clay Verge*; Theodore Roethke: *Praise to the End!* (USA).

1952: W.H. Auden: *Nones*; David Jones: *The Anathemata*; W.R. Rodgers: *Europe and the Bull*; Dylan Thomas: *In Country Sleep*.

1953: C. Day Lewis: *An Italian Visit*; Walter de la Mare: *O Lovely England*; Geoffrey Grigson: *Legenda Suecana*; Theodore Roethke: *The Waking: Poems 1933-1953* (USA).

1954: John Betjeman: *A Few Late Chrysanthemums*; George Barker: *A Vision of Beasts and Gods*; Norman Nicholson: *The Pot Geranium*; F.T. Prince: *Soldiers Bathing*; Jon Silkin: *The Peaceable Kingdom*; Vernon Watkins: *The Death Bell*.

1955: W.H. Auden: *The Shield of Achilles*; Elizabeth Bishop: *A Cold Spring* (USA); W.S. Graham: *The Nightfishing*; Elizabeth Jennings: *A Way of Looking*; Philip Larkin: *The Less Deceived*; Norman MacCaig: *Riding Lights*; Herbert Read: *Moon's Farm*; Wallace Stevens: *Collected Poems* (USA 1954); R.S. Thomas: *Song at the Year's Turning*; Charles Tomlinson: *The Necklace.*

1956: John Ashbery: *Some Trees* (USA); Kingsley Amis: *A Case of Samples*; David Gascoyne: *Night Thoughts*; Allen Ginsberg: *Howl* (USA); Hugh MacDiarmid: *In Memoriam James Joyce*; Edwin Muir: *One Foot in Eden*; Kathleen Raine: *Collected Poems*; Siegfried Sassoon: *Sequences*; E.J. Scovell: *The River Steamer.*

1957: Roy Fuller: *Brutus's Orchard*; Thom Gunn: *The Sense of Movement*; Ted Hughes: *The Hawk in the Rain*; Louis MacNeice: *Visitations*; Stevie Smith: *Not Waving, But Drowning.*

1958: James K. Baxter: *In Fires of No Return* (NZ); Michael Hamburger: *The Dual Site*; Elizabeth Jennings: *A Sense of the World*; Thomas Kinsella: *Another September*; Theodore Roethke: *Words for the Wind* (USA 1957); R.S. Thomas: *Poetry for Supper.*

1959: Geoffrey Hill: *For the Unfallen*; George Mackay Brown: *Loaves and Fishes*; Robert Lowell: *Life Studies* (USA); Peter Redgrove: *The Collector*; Gary Snyder: *Riprap* (USA).

1960: W.H. Auden: *Homage to Clio*; John Betjeman: *Summoned by Bells*; Ted Hughes: *Lupercal*; Patrick Kavanagh: *Come Dance with Kitty Stobling*; Charles Olson: *The Maximus Poems* (USA); Sylvia Plath: *The Colossus*; W.D. Snodgrass: *Heart's Needle* (USA, 1959); Gary Snyder: *Myths and Texts* (USA); Charles Tomlinson: *Seeing Is Believing.*

1961: Thomas Blackburn: *A Smell of Burning*; Austin Clarke: *Later Poems*; Jack Clemo: *The Map of Clay*; H.D.: *Helen in Egypt* (USA); Roy Fisher: *City*; John Fuller: *Fair-ground Music*; Allen Ginsberg: *Kaddish* (USA); Thom Gunn: *My Sad Captains*; Elizabeth Jennings: *Song for a Birth or a Death*; Louis MacNeice: *Solstices*; John Montague: *Poisoned Lands*; Peter Porter: *Once Bitten, Twice Bitten*; Peter Redgrove: *The Nature of Cold Weather*; R.S. Thomas: *Tares.*

1962: John Ashbery: *The Tennis Court Oath* (USA); Robert Graves: *New Poems 1962*; Weldon Kees: *Collected Poems* (USA);* Robert Lowell: *Imitations*; Thomas Kinsella: *Downstream*; Christopher Middleton: *Torse 3*; Derek Walcott: *In a Green Night: Poems 1948-1960*; William Carlos Williams: *Pictures from Brueghel* (USA); James Wright: *The Branch Will Not Break* (USA).

1963: Austin Clarke: *Flight to Africa*; Allen Ginsberg: *Reality Sandwiches* (USA); George MacBeth: *The Broken Places*; Louis MacNeice: *The Burning Perch*;* Richard Murphy: *Sailing to an Island*; William Carlos Williams: *Paterson* (USA); Bernard Spencer: *With Luck Lasting*; Charles Tomlinson: *A Peopled Landscape.*

1964: John Berryman: *77 Dream Songs* (USA); John Betjeman: *A Ring of Bells*; Thomas Blackburn: *A Breathing Space*; Keith Douglas: *Selected Poems*;* Philip Larkin: *The Whitsun Weddings*; Frank O'Hara:

Lunch Poems (USA); Peter Porter: *Poems Ancient and Modern*; Anne Sexton: *Selected Poems* (USA).

1965: Elizabeth Bishop: *Questions of Travel* (USA); Roy Fuller: *Buff*; Denise Levertov: *The Jacob's Ladder* (USA 1961); Peter Levi: *The Shearwaters*; C. Day Lewis: *The Room*; Robert Lowell: *For the Union Dead* (USA); Norman MacCaig: *Measures*; Christopher Middleton: *Nonsequences*; Sylvia Plath: *Ariel*;* Theodore Roethke: *The Far Field* (USA 1964);* Jon Silkin: *Nature with Man*; Gary Snyder: *Riprap and Cold Mountain Poems* (USA); Derek Walcott: *The Castaway*.

1966: John Ashbery: *Rivers and Mountains* (USA); W.H. Auden: *About the House*; James K. Baxter: *Pig Island Letters* (NZ); Basil Bunting: *Briggflatts*; Keith Douglas: *Collected Poems*;* Roy Fisher: *The Ship's Orchestra*; Seamus Heaney: *Death of a Naturalist*; Randall Jarrell: *The Lost World* (USA 1965); Thomas Kinsella: *Wormwood*; Norman MacCaig: *Surroundings*; Peter Redgrove: *The Force*; Anne Sexton: *Live or Die* (USA); Stevie Smith: *The Frog Prince*; Gary Snyder: *Back Country*; R.S. Thomas: *Pietà*; Louis Zukofsky: *'A' 1-12* (USA).

1967: John Ashbery: *Selected Poems* (USA); Martin Bell: *Collected Poems 1937-1966*; Edward Kamau Brathwaite: *Rights of Passage*; Alan Brownjohn: *The Lions' Mouths*; Austin Clarke: *Old-Fashioned Pilgrimage*; Jack Clemo: *Cactus on Carmel*; Robert Garioch: *Collected Poems*; Thom Gunn: *Touch*; Ted Hughes: *Wodwo*; Thomas Kinsella: *Nightwalker*; Robert Lowell: *Near the Ocean* (USA); Roger McGough: *Summer with Monika*; John Montague: *A Chosen Light*; Brian Patten: *Little Johnny's Confession*; Tom Pickard: *High on the Walls*; Gary Snyder: *The Back Country* (USA, 1968); Ken Smith: *The Pity*.

1968: John Berryman: *His Toy, His Dream, His Rest*; Edward Kamau Brathwaite: *Masks*; Basil Bunting: *Collected Poems*; Austin Clarke: *The Echo at Coole*; Peter Dale: *The Storms*; Roy Fuller: *New Poems*; Allen Ginsberg: *Planet News* (USA); Lee Harwood: *The White Room*; Geoffrey Hill: *King Log*; Adrian Henri: *Tonight at Noon*; Thomas Kinsella: *Nightwalker*; Denise Levertov: *The Sorrow Dance* (USA 1967); Norman MacCaig: *Rings on a Tree*; Derek Mahon: *Night Crossing*; Adrian Mitchell: *Out Loud*; Edwin Morgan: *The Second Life*; Marianne Moore: *Complete Poems* (USA, 1967); Richard Murphy: *The Battle of Aughrim*; Lorine Niedecker: *North Central* (USA); J.H. Prynne: *Kitchen Poems*; Tom Raworth: *The Big Green Day*; R.S. Thomas: *Not That He Brought Flowers*.

1969: W.H. Auden: *City Without Walls*; Edward Kamau Brathwaite: *Islands*; Douglas Dunn: *Terry Street*; Roy Fisher: *Collected Poems 1968*; Michael Hamburger: *Travelling*; Seamus Heaney: *Door into the Dark*; Michael Longley: *No Continuing City*; Norman MacCaig: *A Man in My Position*; Brian Patten: *Notes to the Hurrying*

Man; Peter Porter: *A Porter Folio*; J.H. Prynne: *The White Stones*; Anne Sexton: *Love Poems* (USA); Charles Tomlinson: *The Way of a World*; Derek Walcott: *The Gulf*; James Wright: *Shall We Gather at the River* (USA 1968); Louis Zukofsky: *'A' 13-21* (USA).

1970: John Ashbery: *The Double Dream of Spring* (USA); Elizabeth Bishop: *The Complete Poems* (USA); Peter Dale: *Mortal Fire*; W.S. Graham: *Malcolm Mooney's Land*; Ian Hamilton: *The Visit*; Tony Harrison: *The Loiners*; Lee Harwood: *The Sinking Colony*; Ted Hughes: *Crow*; Robert Lowell: *Notebook* (USA 1969); Christopher Middleton: *Our Flowers & Nice Bones*; John Montague: *Tides*; Peter Porter: *The Last of England*.

1971: Fleur Adcock: *High Tide in the Garden*; George Mackay Brown: *Fishermen with Ploughs*; Roy Fisher: *Matrix*; Thom Gunn: *Moly*; Geoffrey Hill: *Mercian Hymns*; Sorley Maclean: *Poems to Eimhir*; Barry MacSweeney: *Our Mutual Scarlet Boulevard*; Sylvia Plath: *Crossing the Water** AND *Winter Trees;** J.H. Prynne: *Brass*; Anne Sexton: *Transformations* (USA); James Simmons: *Energy to Burn*; Gary Snyder: *Regarding Wave* (USA 1970).

1972: Stewart Conn: *An Ear to the Ground*; H.D.: *Hermetic Definition* (USA); Douglas Dunn: *The Happier Life*; D.J. Enright: *Daughters of Earth*; James Fenton: *Terminal Moraine*; Seamus Heaney: *Wintering Out*; Daniel Huws: *Noth*; Thomas Kinsella: *Butcher's Dozen*; Derek Mahon: *Lives*; John Montague: *The Rough Field*; Norman Nicholson: *A Local Habitation*; Peter Porter: *Preaching to the Converted*; Peter Redgrove: *Dr Faust's Sea-Spiral Spirit*; R.S. Thomas: *H'm*; Charles Tomlinson: *Written on Water*; Stevie Smith: *Scorpion.**

1973: James K. Baxter: *Runes* (NZ); Edward Kamau Brathwaite: *The Arrivants: A New World Trilogy*; D.J. Enright: *The Terrible Shears*; Roy Fuller: *Tiny Tears*; Michael Hamburger: *Ownerless Earth*; Michael Longley: *An Exploded View*; Robert Lowell: *The Dolphin* AND *For Lizzie and Harriet* AND *History* (USA); Norman MacCaig: *The White Bird*; Edwin Morgan: *From Glasgow to Saturn*; Adrienne Rich: *Diving into the Wreck* (USA); Derek Walcott: *Another Life*.

1974: Fleur Adcock: *The Scenic Route*; James K. Baxter: *The Labyrinth*; Douglas Dunn: *Love or Nothing*; Geoffrey Grigson: *Angles and Circles*; John Heath-Stubbs: *Artorius* (2nd edition); John Hewitt: *Out of My Time*; David Jones: *The Sleeping Lord;** Jenny Joseph: *Rose in the Afternoon*; Thomas Kinsella: *One*; Philip Larkin: *High Windows*; Richard Murphy: *High Island*; Douglas Oliver: *In the Cave of Suicession*; C.H. Sisson: *In the Trojan Ditch: Collected Poems*; Anne Sexton: *The Book of Folly* (USA 1972); James Simmons: *West Strand Visions*; Gary Snyder: *Turtle Island* (USA); Anne Stevenson: *Correspondences* AND *Travelling Behind Glass*; Charles Tomlinson: *The Way In*.

1975: John Ashbery: *Self-Portrait in a Convex Mirror* (USA); Frances Bellerby: *The First-Known*; James Berry: *Lucy's Letter*; Jeni Couzyn: *Christmas in Africa*; D.J. Enright: *Sad Ires*; Roy Fuller: *From the Joke Shop*; Robert Graves: *Collected Poems*; Michael Hartnett: *A Farewell to English*; Seamus Heaney: *North*; Ted Hughes: *Cave Birds*; Linton Kwesi Johnson: *Dread, Beat and Blood*; Thomas Kinsella: *New Poems*; Derek Mahon: *The Snow Party*; Christopher Middleton: *The Lonely Suppers of W.V. Balloon*; John Montague: *A Slow Dance*; George Oppen: *The Collected Poems of George Oppen, 1929-1975* (USA); Peter Porter: *Living in a Calm Country*; Peter Scupham: *Prehistories*; Anne Sexton: *The Death Notebooks* (USA 1974).

1976: James K. Baxter: *The Bone Chanter* (NZ); Elizabeth Bishop: *Geography III* (USA); Veronica Forrest-Thomson: *On the Periphery*;*; Thom Gunn: *Jack Straw's Castle*; John Hewitt: *Time Enough*; Peter Levi: *Collected Poems 1955-1975*; Michael Longley: *Man Lying on a Wall*; Christopher Middleton: *Pataxanadu*; R.S. Thomas: *Laboratories of the Spirit*; Derek Walcott: *Sea Grapes*.

1977: John Ashbery: *Houseboat Days* (USA) AND *Three Poems* (USA 1972); Edward Kamau Brathwaite: *Mother Poem*; Elaine Feinstein: *Some Unease and Angels*; W.S. Graham: *Implements in Their Places*; Michael Hamburger: *Real Estate*; Anthony Hecht: *Millions of Strange Shadows* (USA); Ted Hughes: *Season Songs*; Edwin Morgan: *The New Divan*; Paul Muldoon: *Mules*; Frank Ormsby: *A Store of Candles*; Tom Paulin: *A State of Justice*; Peter Reading: *Nothing for Anyone*; Peter Scupham: *The Hinterland*; Anne Stevenson: *Enough of Green*; Kit Wright: *The Bear Looked Over the Mountain*.

1978: Peter Dale: *One Another*; D.J. Enright: *Paradise Illustrated*; U.A. Fanthorpe: *Side Effects*; Roy Fisher: *The Thing About Joe Sullivan*; Tony Harrison: *From 'The School of Eloquence'*; Lee Harwood: *Crossing the Frozen River*; John Hewitt: *The Rain Dance*; Geoffrey Hill: *Tenebrae*; Jenny Joseph: *The Thinking Heart*; Robert Lowell: *Day by Day* (USA 1977); Hugh MacDiarmid: *Complete Poems 1920-1976*;* Sorley Maclean (Somhairle MacGill-Eain): *Springtide and Neaptide*; Barry MacSweeney: *Odes*; John Montague: *The Great Cloak*; Andrew Motion: *The Pleasure Steamers*; Philip Pacey: *Charged Landscapes*; Peter Porter: *The Cost of Seriousness*; Craig Raine: *The Onion, Memory*; Adrienne Rich: *The Dream of a Common Language* (USA); R.S. Thomas: *Frequencies*; Charles Tomlinson: *The Shaft*; Jeffrey Wainwright: *Heart's Desire*; Louis Zukofsky: *'A'-22 & 23* (USA 1975) AND *'A'*, complete version (USA).*

1979: Fleur Adcock: *The Inner Harbour*; John Ashbery: *As We Know* (USA); James Berry: *Fractured Circles*; Keith Douglas: *Complete Poems*;* W.S. Graham: *Collected Poems 1949-1977*; Douglas Dunn:

Barbarians; D.J. Enright: *A Faust Book*; John Fuller: *Lies and Secrets*; Seamus Heaney: *Field Work*; Ted Hughes: *Moortown* AND *Remains of Elmet*; Thomas Kinsella: *Fifteen Dead* AND *One and Other Poems*; Michael Longley: *The Echo Gate*; Derek Mahon: *Poems 1962-1978*; Christopher Middleton: *Carminalenia*; Craig Raine: *A Martian Sends a Postcard Home*; Peter Reading: *Fiction*; Peter Redgrove: *The Weddings at Nether Powers*; Christopher Reid: *Arcadia*; George Szirtes: *The Slant Door*; Terence Tiller: *That Singing Mesh*; James Wright: *To a Blossoming Pear Tree* (USA 1977).

1980: David Constantine: *A Brightness to Cast Shadows*; Ruth Fainlight: *Sibyls and Others*; Roy Fisher: *Poems 1975-1980*; John Fuller: *The Illusionists*; Roy Fuller: *The Reign of Sparrows*; Anthony Hecht: *The Venetian Vespers* (USA 1979); Frances Horovitz: *Water Over Stone*; Linton Kwesi Johnson: *Inglan is a Bitch*; George Mac-Beth: *Poems of Love and Death*; Paul Muldoon: *Why Brownlee Left*; Tom Paulin: *The Strange Museum*; John Riley: *The Collected Works*;* Peter Scupham: *Summer Palaces*; Penelope Shuttle: *The Orchard Upstairs*; James Simmons: *Constantly Singing*; C.H. Sisson: *Exactions*; Derek Walcott: *The Star-Apple Kingdom* (USA 1979).

1981: Alison Brackenbury: *Dreams of Power*; Douglas Dunn: *St Kilda's Parliament*; Vicki Feaver: *Close Relatives*; Tony Harrison: *Continuous*; Libby Houston: *At the Mercy*; Christopher Logue: *War Music*; Andrew Motion: *Independence*; Norman Nicholson: *Sea to the West*; Peter Reading: *Tom O'Bedlam's Beauties*; Peter Redgrove: *The Apple-Broadcast*; Carol Rumens: *Unplayed Music*; Ken Smith: *Fox Running*; George Szirtes: *November and May*; R.S. Thomas: *Between Here and Now*; Charles Tomlinson: *The Flood*.

1982: John Ash: *The Goodbyes*; John Ashbery: *Shadow Train* (USA 1981); Edward Kamau Brathwaite: *Sun Poem*; John Cassidy: *Night Cries*; Gillian Clarke: *Letter from a Far Country*; Peter Didsbury: *The Butchers of Hull*; Paul Durcan: *The Selected Paul Durcan*; U.A. Fanthorpe: *Standing To*; James Fenton: *The Memory of War*; Thom Gunn: *The Passages of Joy*; Sue Lenier: *Swansong*; Medbh McGuckian: *The Flower Master*; Derek Mahon: *The Hunt by Night*; Les A. Murray: *The Vernacular Republic* (AUSTRALIA 1976); J.H. Prynne: *Poems*; E.J. Scovell: *The Space Between*; Ken Smith: *The Poet Reclining: Selected Poems 1962-1980*; Anne Stevenson: *Minute by Glass Minute*; Derek Walcott: *The Fortunate Traveller* (USA 1981).

1983: Elizabeth Bishop: *Complete Poems 1927-1979* (USA);* David Constantine: *Watching for Dolphins*; Ruth Fainlight: *Fifteen to Infinity*; James Fenton: *Children in Exile*; Carolyn Forché: *The Country Between Us* (USA 1981); John Fuller: *The Beautiful Inventions*; Geoffrey Hill: *The Mystery of the Charity of Charles Péguy*; Michael Hofmann: *Nights in the Iron Hotel*; Frances Horovitz: *Snow Light, Water Light*; Ted Hughes: *River*; Jenny Joseph: *Beyond Descartes*; Norman MacCaig: *A World of Difference*; Christopher Middleton: *111 Poems*; Andrew Motion: *Secret Narratives*; Paul Muldoon: *Quoof*; Grace Nichols: *I is a long-memoried woman*; Sean O'Brien: *The Indoor Park*; Tom Paulin: *Liberty Tree*; Peter Reading: *Diplopic*; Carol Rumens: *Star Whisper*; Peter Scupham: *Winter Quarters*; Gary Snyder: *Axe-Handles* (USA); George Szirtes: *Short Wave*; Gael Turnbull: *A Gathering of Poems 1950-1980*; Kit Wright: *Bump-Starting the Hearse*.

1984: John Ash: *The Branching Stairs*; John Ashbery: *A Wave* (USA); Amy Clampitt: *The Kingfisher* (USA 1983); U.A Fanthorpe: *Voices Off*; Alison Fell: *Kisses for Mayakovsky*; Geoffrey Grigson: *Montaigne's Tower*; Philip Gross: *The Ice Factory*; Tony Harrison: *Selected Poems*; Seamus Heaney: *Sweeney Astray* (IRELAND 1983) AND *Station Island*; Selima Hill: *Saying Hello at the Station*; Frank Kuppner: *A Bad Day for the Sung Dynasty*; Tom Leonard: *Intimate Voices*; Liz Lochhead: *Dreaming Frankenstein*; E.A. Markham: *Human Rites*; Medbh McGuckian: *Venus and the Rain*; John Montague: *The Dead Kingdom*; Blake Morrison: *Dark Glasses*; Grace Nichols: *The Fat Black Woman's Poems*; Peter Porter: *Fast Forward*; Craig Raine: *Rich*; Tom Raworth: *Tottering State*; Peter Reading: *C*; Jeremy Reed: *By the Fisheries*; David Scott: *A Quiet Gathering*; Iain Crichton Smith: *The Exiles*; Derek Walcott: *Midsummer*.

1985: James Berry: *Chain of Days*; Fred D'Aguiar: *Mama Dot*; Douglas Dunn: *Elegies*; Tony Harrison: *v.*; Carol Ann Duffy: *Standing Female Nude*; Paul Durcan: *The Berlin Wall Café*; D.J. Enright: *Instant Chronicles*; Sylvia Kantaris: *The Sea at the Door*; Jenny Joseph: *Persephone*; Derek Mahon: *Antarctica*; Richard Murphy: *The Price of Stone*; Douglas Oliver: *The Infant and the Pearl*; Peter Reading: *Ukelele Music*; Oliver Reynolds: *Skevington's Daughter*; Carol Rumens: *Direct Dialling*; William Scammell: *Jouissance*; Anne Stevenson: *The Fiction-Makers*; Matthew Sweeney: *The Lame Waltzer*; Hugo Williams: *Writing Home*; Benjamin Zephaniah: *The Dread Affair*.

1986: Fleur Adcock: *The Incident Book*; Amy Clampitt: *What the Light Was Like* (USA 1985); John Cooper Clarke: *10 Years in an Open-Necked Shirt*; Wendy Cope: *Making Cocoa for Kingsley Amis*; Nuala Ní Dhomhnaill: *Selected Poems*; Roy Fisher: *A Furnace*; Denise Levertov: *Selected Poems* (USA) AND *Oblique Prayers* (USA 1984); Michael Hofmann: *Acrimony*; Michael Horovitz: *Midsummer Morning Jog Log*; E.A. Markham: *Living in Disguise*; Christopher Middleton: *Two Horse Wagon Going By*; Frank Ormsby: *A Northern Spring*; Fiona Pitt-Kethley: *Sky Ray Lolly*; Peter Reading: *Stet*; Stephen Romer: *Idols*; Vikram Seth: *The Golden Gate* (USA/INDIA); Ken Smith: *Terra*;

Michael Smith: *It A Come*;* George Szirtes: *The Photographer in Winter*; R.S. Thomas: *Experimenting with an Amen*.

1987: Gillian Allnutt: *Beginning the Avocado*; John Ash: *Disbelief*; Edward Kamau Brathwaite: *X/ Self*; Eavan Boland: *The Journey*; David Constantine: *Madder*; Peter Didsbury: *The Classical Farm*; Carol Ann Duffy: *Selling Manhattan*; Paul Durcan: *Going Home to Russia*; Jean Earle: *Visiting Light*; U.A. Fanthorpe: *A Watching Brief*; Seamus Heaney: *The Haw Lantern*; Jeremy Hooker: *Master of the Leaping Figures*; Kathleen Jamie: *The Way We Live*; Brendan Kennelly: *Cromwell* (IRELAND 1983); Paul Muldoon: *Meeting the British*; Blake Morrison: *The Ballad of the Yorkshire Ripper*; Sean O'Brien: *The Frighteners*; Douglas Oliver: *Kind*; Tom Paulin: *Fivemiletown*; Peter Porter: *The Automatic Oracle*; Peter Redgrove: *In the Hall of the Saurians*; Oliver Reynolds: *The Player Queen's Wife*; Carole Satyamurti: *Broken Moon*; Peter Sirr: *Talk, Talk*; Ken Smith: *Wormwood*; R.S. Thomas: *The Echoes Return Slow*; Charles Tomlinson: *The Return*; John Hartley Williams: *Bright River Yonder*.

1988: John Ashbery: *April Galleons* (USA); Sujata Bhatt: *Brunizem*; Jean Binta Breeze: *Riddym Ravings*; Ciaran Carson: *The Irish for No* (IRELAND 1987); Michael Donaghy: *Shibboleth* (USA); Helen Dunmore: *The Raw Garden*; Douglas Dunn: *Northlight*; John Fuller: *The Grey Among the Green*; Philip Gross & Sylvia Kantaris: *The Air Mines of Mistila*; Selima Hill: *My Darling Camel*; Mick Imlah: *Birthmarks*; Alan Jenkins: *In the Hot-House*; Thomas Kinsella: *Blood and Family*; Denise Levertov: *Breathing the Water* (USA 1987); Medbh McGuckian: *On Ballycastle Beach*; Lachlan Mackinnon: *Monterey Express*; Les Murray: *The Daylight Moon* (AUSTRALIA); Peter Reading: *Final Demands*; Peter Scupham: *The Air Show*; Jo Shapcott: *Electroplating the Baby*; Penelope Shuttle: *Adventures with My Horse*; George Szirtes: *Metro*; Adam Thorpe: *Nights in the Baltic*; Derek Walcott: *The Arkansas Testament* (USA 1987); C.K. Williams: *Poems 1963-1983* (USA) AND *Flesh and Blood* (USA 1987); Heathcote Williams: *Whale Nation*.

1989: Simon Armitage: *Zoom!*; Gillian Clarke: *Letting in the Rumour*; Fred D'Aguiar: *Airy Hall*; James Fenton: *Manila Envelope* (PHILIPPINES); Roy Fuller: *Available for Dreams*; Selima Hill: *The Accumulation of Small Acts of Kindness*; Ted Hughes: *Wolfwatching*; John Montague: *Mount Eagle* (IRELAND 1988); Richard Murphy: *The Mirror Wall*; Les Murray: *The Boys Who Stole the Funeral* (AUSTRALIA 1979); Peter Reading: *Perduta Gente*; Carol Rumens: *From Berlin to Heaven*; Iain Sinclair: *Flesh Eggs & Scalp Metal*; Iain Crichton Smith: *The Village*; Pauline Stainer: *The Honeycomb*; Matthew Sweeney: *Blue Shoes*; Charles Tomlinson: *Annunciations*; Kit Wright: *Short Afternoons*.

1990: Eavan Boland: *Outside History*; Ciaran Carson: *Belfast Con-*

fetti (IRELAND 1989); Robert Crawford: *A Scottish Assembly*; Allen Curnow: *Selected Poems 1940-1989*; Nuala Ní Dhomhnaill: *Pharoah's Daughter*; Carol Ann Duffy: *The Other Country*; Paul Durcan: *Daddy, Daddy*; Andrew Greig: *The Order of the Day*; Glyn Maxwell: *Tale of the Mayor's Son*; Paul Muldoon: *Madoc*; Ken Smith: *The heart, the border*; Anne Stevenson: *The Other House*; Adam Thorpe: *Meeting Montaigne*; R.S. Thomas: *Counterpoint*; Derek Walcott: *Omeros*.

1991: Fleur Adcock: *Time-Zones*; John Ash: *The Burnt Pages*; John Ashbery: *Flow Chart* (USA); Margaret Atwood: *Poems 1965-1975* (CANADA, 1976); Sujata Bhatt: *Monkey Shadows*; John Burnside: *Common Knowledge*; Stephen Dobyns: *Cemetery Nights* (USA 1987); Maura Dooley: *Explaining Magnetism*; Ian Duhig: *The Bradford Count*; Paul Durcan: *Crazy About Women*; G.F. Dutton: *The Concrete Garden*; Elizabeth Garrett: *The Rule of Three*; Dana Gioia: *The Gods of Winter* (USA); Tony Harrison: *A Cold Coming*; Seamus Heaney: *Seeing Things*; Linton Kwesi Johnson: *Tings an Times*; Jackie Kay: *The Adoption Papers*; Brendan Kennelly: *The Book of Judas*; Mimi Khalvati: *In White Ink*; Christopher Logue: *Kings*; Michael Longley: *Gorse Fires*; Paula Meehan: *The Man Who Was Marked by Winter*; David Morley: *The Mandelstam Variations*; Les Murray: *Dog Fox Field* (AUSTRALIA); Sean O'Brien: *HMS Glasshouse*; Julie O'Callaghan: *What's What*; Bernard O'Donoghue: *The Weakness*; Michèle Roberts: *Psyche and the Hurricane*; Harry Smart: *Pierrot*; George Szirtes: *Bridge Passages*; Gerard Woodward: *Householder*; Fred Voss: *Goodstone* (USA).

1992: John Ashbery: *Hotel Lautréamont* (USA); Simon Armitage: *Kid* AND *Xanadu*; Margaret Atwood: *Poems 1975-1986* (USA 1987); Kamau Brathwaite: *Middle Passages*; Jean Binta Breeze: *Spring Cleaning*; John Burnside: *Feast Days*; Wendy Cope: *Serious Concerns*; Robert Crawford: *Talkies*; Nuala Ní Dhomhnaill: *The Astrakhan Cloak*; U.A. Fanthorpe: *Neck-Verse*; Thom Gunn: *The Man with Night Sweats*; Tony Harrison: *The Gaze of the Gorgon*; Ted Hughes: *Rain-Charm for the Duchy and Other Laureate Poems*; Glyn Maxwell: *Out of the Rain*; Medbh McGuckian: *Marconi's Cottage* (IRELAND 1991); Christopher Middleton: *The Balcony Tree*; Peter Porter: *The Chair of Babel*; Peter Reading: *Evagatory*; Stephen Romer: *Plato's Ladder*; Jo Shapcott: *Phrase Book*; Pauline Stainer: *Sighting the Slave Ship*; Matthew Sweeney: *Cacti*; R.S. Thomas: *Mass for Hard Times*; Chase Twichell: *Perdido* (USA 1991); Susan Wicks: *Singing Under Water*; C.K. Williams: *A Dream of Mind* (USA); David Wright: *Poems and Versions*; Benjamin Zephaniah: *City Psalms*.

1993: Moniza Alvi: *The Country at My Shoulder*; Simon Armitage: *Book of Matches*; Patricia Beer: *Friend of Heraclitus*; Charles Boyle: *The Very Man*; Ciaran Carson: *First Language*; Gillian Clarke: *The*

King of Britain's Daughter; Michael Donaghy: *Errata*; Carol Ann Duffy: *Mean Time*; Paul Durcan: *A Snail in My Prime*; James Fenton: *Out of Danger*; Lavinia Greenlaw: *Night Photograph*; Selima Hill: *A Little Book of Meat*; Nicki Jackowska: *News from the Brighton Front*; Kathleen Jamie: *The Autonomous Region*; Jackie Kay: *Other Lovers*; Stephen Knight: *Flowering Limbs*; Jamie McKendrick: *The Kiosk on the Brink*; John Montague: *Time in Armagh*; Les Murray: *Translations from the Natural World* (AUSTRALIA); Sharon Olds: *The Father* (USA); Ruth Padel: *Angel*; Don Paterson: *Nil Nil*; Anne Rouse: *Sunset Grill*; Ken Smith: *Tender to the Queen of Spain*; Anne Stevenson: *Four and a Half Dancing Men*.

1994: Gillian Allnutt: *Blackthorn*; Eavan Boland: *In a Time of Violence*; John Burnside: *The Myth of the Twin*; David Constantine: *Caspar Hauser*; Kwame Dawes: *Progeny of Air*; Peter Didsbury: *That Old-Time Religion*; Helen Dunmore: *Recovering a Body*; Paul Durcan: *Give Me Your Hand*; Ruth Fainlight: *This Time of Year*; Vicki Feaver: *The Handless Maiden*; Roy Fisher: *Birmingham River*; Carolyn Forché: *The Angel of History* (USA 1993); Linda France: *The Gentleness of the Very Tall*; Ida Affleck Graves: *A Kind Husband*; W.N. Herbert: *Forked Tongue*; Kathleen Jamie: *The Queen of Sheba*; Alan Jenkins: *Harm*; Thomas Kinsella: *From Centre City*; Ian McMillan: *Dad, the Donkey's on Fire*; Paula Meehan: *Pillow Talk*; Paul Muldoon: *The Annals of Chile*; Douglas Oliver: *Penniless Politics*; Craig Raine: *History: The Home Movie*; Peter Reading: *Last Poems*; Deryn Rees-Jones: *The Memory Tray*; Peter Sansom: *January*; Carol Satyamurti: *Striking Distance*; Iain Crichton Smith: *Ends and Beginnings*; Pauline Stainer: *The Ice-Pilot Speaks*; George Szirtes: *Blind Field*; Hugo Williams: *Dock Leaves*; Gerard Woodward: *After the Deafening*.

1995: Simon Armitage: *The Dead Sea Poems*; James Berry: *Hot Earth Cold Earth*; Sujata Bhatt: *The Stinking Rose*; John Burnside: *Swimming in the Flood*; Kate Clanchy: *Slattern*; Julia Copus: *The Shuttered Eye*; Mark Doty: *My Alexandria*; Ian Duhig: *The Mersey Goldfish*; Jane Duran: *Breathe Now, Breathe*; U.A. Fanthorpe: *Safe as Houses*; Sophie Hannah: *The Hero and the Girl Next Door*; Maggie Hannan: *Liar, Jones*; Brendan Kennelly: *Poetry My Arse*; Mimi Khalvati: *Mirrorwork*; Jenny Joseph: *Ghosts and other company*; James Lasdun: *The Revenant*; Gwyneth Lewis: *Parables & Faxes*; Michael Longley: *The Ghost Orchid*; Medbh McGuckian: *Captain Lavender*; Glyn Maxwell: *Rest for the Wicked*; Sean O'Brien: *Ghost Train*; Bernard O'Donoghue: *Gunpowder*; Katherine Pierpoint: *Truffle Beds*; Milner Place: *In a Rare Time of Rain*; Justin Quinn: *The 'O'o'a'a' Bird*; Maurice Riordan: *A Word from the Loki*; Carol Rumens: *Best China Sky*; R.S. Thomas: *No Truce with the Furies*.

Anthologies

MODERN / CONTEMPORARY
(in approximate historical order. † = now out of print)

Michael Roberts: *The Faber Book of Modern Verse* (1936; 4th edition revised 1982 by Peter Porter).

Kenneth Allott: *English Poetry 1918-1960* (revised 1962 version of *The Penguin Book of Contemporary Verse*, 1950).

John Heath-Stubbs & David Wright: *The Faber Book of 20th Century Verse* (1953; 3rd edition 1975).

George MacBeth: *Poetry 1900 to 1975* (Longman, 1979; revised version of *Poetry 1900 to 1965* [Longman/Faber, 1967]).

Philip Larkin: *The Oxford Book of 20th Century Verse* (1973).

Ian Hamilton: *The Poetry of War, 1939-45*† (Alan Ross, 1965).

Brian Gardner: *The Terrible Rain: Poets 1939-1945* (Methuen, 1966).

Catherine Reilly: *Chaos of the Night: Women's Poetry and Verse of the Second World War* (Virago, 1984).

The Oasis Selection: *Poems of the Second World War* (Dent, 1985) AND *More Poems of the Second World War* (Dent, 1989).

Robin Skelton: *Poetry of the Forties* (Penguin, 1968).

D.J. Enright: *Poets of the 1950s: An Anthology of New English Verse*† (Kenkyusha, Tokyo, 1955).

Dannie Abse: *Mavericks*† (Editions Poetry and Poverty, 1957).

Robert Conquest: *New Lines*† (Macmillan, 1957) AND *New Lines II*† (Macmillan, 1963).

Philip Hobsbaum & Edward Lucie-Smith: *A Group Anthology*† (OUP, 1963).

A. Alvarez: *The New Poetry* (Penguin, 1962; revised 1966).

David Wright: *Longer Contemporary Poems*† (Penguin, 1966).

Michael Horovitz: *Children of Albion: Poetry of the 'Underground' in Britain*† (Penguin, 1969).

Edward Lucie-Smith: *British Poetry Since 1945* (Penguin, 1970; revised 1985).

Jeremy Robson: *The Young British Poets*† (Chatto, 1971).

Jon Silkin: *Poetry of the Committed Individual: a* Stand *anthology of poetry*† (Gollancz/Penguin, 1973).

Edward B. Germain: *English and American Surrealist Poetry* (Penguin, 1978).

D.J. Enright: *The Oxford Book of Contemporary Verse* (OUP, 1980).

Blake Morrison & Andrew Motion: *The Penguin Book of Contemporary British Poetry* (1982).

Michael Schmidt: *Some Contemporary Poets of Britain and Ireland* (Carcanet, 1983).

Sylvia Paskin, Jay Ramsay & Jeremy Silver: *Angels of Fire: An Anthology of Radical Poetry in the '80s* (Chatto, 1986).

Andrew Crozier & Tim Longville: *A Various Art* (Carcanet, 1987; paperback edition Paladin 1990).

Jonathan Barker: *Thirty Years of the Poetry Book Society* (Poetry Book Society/Hutchinson, 1988).

Gillian Allnutt, Fred D'Aguiar, Ken Edwards & Eric Mottram: *The New British Poetry* (Paladin, 1988).

Neil Astley: *Poetry with an Edge* (Bloodaxe, 1988).

Dannie Abse: *The Hutchinson Book of Post-War British Poets* (1989).

Gordon Brown: *High on the Walls: a Morden Tower anthology* (Morden Tower/Bloodaxe, 1990).

W.R. Owens: *The Poetry Anthology: Literature in the Modern World* (Open University, 1991).

Michael Horovitz: *Grandchildren of Albion* (New Departures, 1992).

Paul Beasley: *The Popular Front of Contemporary Poetry Anthology* (Apples & Snakes, 1992).

Michael Hulse, David Kennedy & David Morley: *The New Poetry* (Bloodaxe, 1993).

Paul Green: *Ten British Poets* (Spectacular Diseases, 1993).

Michael Schmidt: *New Poetries* (Carcanet, 1994).

Judi Benson & Agneta Falk: *The Long Pale Corridor: contemporary poems of bereavement* (Bloodaxe, 1996).

SERIES

New Poems: The P.E.N. Anthologies of Contemporary Poetry† (Michael Joseph, 1952-58; Hutchinson, 1960-77).

New Poetry, 1–9† (Arts Council, 1975-77; Arts Council/P.E.N./Hutchinson, 1978-83).

P.E.N. New Poetry, 1 & 2 (Quartet, 1986 & 1988).

Penguin Modern Poets, 1–27 (Penguin, 1962–79).

Penguin Modern Poets, new series, 1– (Penguin, 1995–).

Penguin Modern European Poets (Penguin, 1960s–70s).

Corgi Modern Poets, 1–5,† ed. Dannie Abse (Corgi, 1971-73).

Poetry Dimension: The Best of the Poetry Year, 1–6,† ed. Dannie Abse & Jeremy Robson (Robson/Abacus, 1973-79).

Poetry Supplement (Poetry Book Society, 1957-85); *Poetry Book Society Anthology* (Poetry Book Society/Hutchinson, 1986-92).

The Gregory Anthology (Secker, 1980; Carcanet, 1981/82; Salamander, 1983/84; Penguin, 1985/86; Hutchinson, 1987/90; Sinclair-Stevenson, 1991-93).

Poetry Introduction, 1–8 (Faber, 1969-93).

New Chatto Poets, 1 & 2 (Chatto, 1986 & 1989).

Raven Introductions, 1–6 (Raven Arts, Dublin, 1981-91).
Peterloo Preview, 1, 2, 3 (Peterloo, 1988, 1990, 1993).
Seren Poets, 1 & 2 (Seren, 1989 & 1991); 1 is called *The Bloodstream*.
Trio 1–7 (Blackstaff, 1980-92).
Northern Poetry, 1 & 2 (Littlewood, 1989 & 1991).
Anvil New Poets, 1 & 2 (Anvil Press, 1990 & 1995).
Re/Active Anthologies, 1–3 (Paladin, 1992).
Forward Book of Poetry (Forward Publishing, 1992–).
Flambard New Poets, 1 & 2 (Flambard, 1993 & 1994).

IRELAND

Dermot Bolger: *The Bright Wave/*An Tonn Gheal: *poetry in Irish now* (Raven, 1986).
Patrick Crotty: *Modern Irish Poetry* (Blackstaff, 1995).
Gerald Dawe: *The New Younger Irish Poets* (Blackstaff, 1982; revised 1991).
John F. Deane: *Dedalus Irish Poets* (Dedalus, 1992).
Seamus Deane: *The Field Day Anthology of Irish Writing*, vols. 1–3 (Field Day Publications, Derry, 1991).
Seán Dunne: *Poets of Munster* (Anvil/Brandon, 1985).
Peter Fallon & Derek Mahon: *The Penguin Book of Contemporary Irish Poetry* (1990).
Padraic Fiacc: *The Wearing of the Black* (Blackstaff, 1974).
Gabriel Fitzmaurice: *Irish Poetry Now* (Wolfhound, 1993).
Brendan Kennelly: *The Penguin Book of Irish Verse* (1970; revised 1972 & 1981).
Thomas Kinsella: *The New Oxford Book of Irish Verse* (1986).
David Marcus: *Irish Poets 1924-1974*† (Pan, 1975).
John Montague: *The Faber Book of Irish Verse* (1974).
John Montague: *Bitter Harvest* (Scribner's, New York, 1989).
Paul Muldoon: *The Faber Book of Contemporary Irish Poetry* (1986).
Frank Ormsby: *Poets from the North of Ireland* (Blackstaff, 1989; revised 1990).
Frank Ormsby: *A Rage for Order: Poetry of the Northern Ireland Troubles* (Blackstaff, 1992).

SCOTLAND

Robin Bell: *The Best of Scottish Poetry* (Chambers, 1989).
Robert Crawford: *Other Tongues: Young Scottish Poets in English, Scots & Gaelic* (Verse, 1990).
Douglas Dunn: *The Faber Book of 20th Century Scottish Poetry* (1992)
Fresh Oceans: an anthology of poetry by Scottish women (Strathmullion, 1989).

Robert Garioch: *Made in Scotland*† (Carcanet, 1974).

Duncan Glen: *Twenty of the Best and One More for Good Measure* (Galliard, 1990).

Charles King & Iain Crichton Smith: *Twelve Modern Scottish Poets* (Hodder, 1971); *Twelve More Modern Scottish Poets* (Hodder, 1986).

Maurice Lindsay: *Modern Scottish Poetry: anthology of the Scottish Renaissance, 1925-1975*† (Carcanet, 1976).

Donald MacAulay: *Nua-Bhardachd Ghàidhlig/Modern Scottish Gaelic Poems*† (Canongate, 1976).

Daniel O'Rourke: *Dream State: The New Scottish Poets* (Polygon, 1994).

Hamish Whyte: *Noise and Smoky Breath: An Illustrated Anthology of Glasgow Poems 1900-1983* (Third Eye, 1983).

Hamish Whyte: *In the Face of Eternity: Eight Gaelic Poets* (Polygon, 1991).

General Scottish anthologies featuring contemporary poetry include:

Tom Scott: *The Penguin Book of Scottish Verse* (1970) and John Mac-Queen & Tom Scott: *The Oxford Book of Scottish Verse* (1966).

WALES

Sam Adams: *Ten Anglo-Welsh Poets*† (Carcanet, 1974).

Cary Archard: *Poetry Wales: 25 Years* (Seren, 1991).

Jude Brigley: *Exchanges* (Honno, 1990).

Tony Curtis: *Love from Wales* (Seren, 1992).

Don Dale-Jones & Randal Jenkins: *Ten Modern Anglo-Welsh Poets* (University of London Press, 1975).

Raymond Garlick & Roland Mathias: *Anglo-Welsh Poetry 1480-1980* (Poetry Wales Press/Seren Books, 1984).

Meic Stephens & Peter Finch: *Green Horse: an anthology by young poets of Wales* (Christopher Davies, 1978).

Meic Stephens: *The Bright Field* (Carcanet, 1991).

ENGLAND

Neil Astley: *Ten North-East Poets* (Bloodaxe, 1980).

Douglas Dunn: *A Rumoured City: new poets from Hull*† (Bloodaxe, 1982).

Adrian Henri, Roger McGough & Brian Patten: *Penguin Modern Poets 10: The Mersey Sound* (Penguin, 1967) AND *New Volume* (Penguin, 1983).

William Scammell: *The New Lake Poets* (Bloodaxe, 1991).

Michael Schmidt: *Ten English Poets*† (Carcanet, 1976).

AMERICA

Donald M. Allen: *The New American Poetry* (Grove, NY, 1960).

James Atlas: *Ten American Poets*† (Carcanet, 1973).

Nina Baym & others: *The Norton Anthology of American Literature*, 2 vols (1979; 3rd edition 1989).

Richard Ellmann: *The New Oxford Book of American Verse* (1976).

Donald Hall: *Contemporary American Poetry* (Penguin, 1962; revised 1972).

Donald Hall: *American Poetry: an introductory anthology* (Faber, 1969).

Geoffrey Moore: *The Penguin Book of American Verse* (1977).

A. Poulin Jr: *Contemporary American Poetry* (Houghton Mifflin, 1971; 4th ed. 1985).

Michael Schmidt: *Five American Poets*† (Carcanet, 1979).

Dave Smith & David Bottoms: *The Morrow Anthology of Younger American Poets* (William Morrow, NY, 1985).

Helen Vendler: *The Faber Book of Contemporary American Poetry* (1986; USA 1985).

EUROPE

A. Alvarez: *The Faber Book of Modern European Poetry* (1992).

Stanley Burnshaw: *The Poem Itself: 150 European poets translated and analysed*† (1960; first UK edition Penguin, 1964).

Michael March: *Child of Europe: a new anthology of East European poetry* (Penguin, 1990).

George Steiner: *The Penguin Book of Modern Verse Translation*† (1966).

Daniel Weissbort: *The Poetry of Survival: Post-War Poets of Central and Eastern Europe* (Anvil, 1991).

See also various anthologies of poetry from different European countries published by Bloodaxe, Forest and Penguin.

AUSTRALIA

Les Murray: *FiveFathers* (Carcanet, 1994).

John Tranter & Philip Mead: *The Bloodaxe Book of Modern Australian Poetry* (Bloodaxe, 1994).

WOMEN

Fleur Adcock: *The Faber Book of 20th Century Women's Poetry* (1987).

Jeni Couzyn: *The Bloodaxe Book of Contemporary Women Poets* (1985).

C. McEwen: *Naming the Waves: Lesbian Poetry* (Virago, 1988).

Rosemary Palmeira: *In the Gold of Flesh* (Women's Press, 1990).

Marge Piercy: *Early Ripening: American Women's Poetry Now* (Pandora, 1987).

The Raving Beauties: *In the Pink* AND *No Holds Barred* (Women's Press, 1983 & 1985).

Carol Rumens: *Making for the Open: The Chatto Book of Post-Feminist Poetry 1964-1984* (1985).

Carol Rumens: *New Women Poets* (Bloodaxe, 1990).

Carol Ann Duffy: *I Wouldn't Thank You for a Valentine* (Viking, 1992).

Linda France: *Sixty Women Poets* (Bloodaxe, 1993).

Melanie Silgardo & Janet Deck: *New Virago Poets* (Virago, 1994).

The Poetry Virgins: *Sauce* (Bloodaxe, 1994).

General women's anthologies featuring contemporary poetry include: Carol Cosman, Joan Keefe and Kathleen Weaver, *The Penguin Book of Women Poets* (1978)†; Louise Bernikow, *The World Split Open: Women Poets 1552-1950* (Women's Press, 1979); Diana Scott: *Bread and Roses: 19th and 20th Century Women's Poetry* (Virago, 1982).

BLACK BRITISH & CARIBBEAN

James Berry: *Bluefoot Traveller*† (Limestone, 1976; revised edition Harrap, 1981).

James Berry: *News for Babylon: The Chatto Book of Westindian-British Poetry* (1984); new enlarged edition due from Bloodaxe, 1997 (co-edited with Mahmood Jamal).

Stewart Brown: *Caribbean Poetry Now* (Hodder, 1984; new ed. 1992).

Stewart Brown, Mervyn Morris & Gordon Rohlehr: *Voiceprint: an anthology of oral and related poetry* (Longman, 1989).

Paula Burnett: *The Penguin Book of Caribbean Verse in English* (1986).

Rhonda Cobham & Merle Collins: *Watchers & Seekers: Creative Writing by Black Women in Britain* (Women's Press, 1987).

Farrukh Dhondy: *Ranters, Ravers and Rhymers: poems by Black and Asian Poets* (Collins, 1990).

E.A. Markham: *Hinterland: Caribbean Poetry from the West Indies & Britain* (Bloodaxe, 1989).

Poems of Our Time

(long poems and sequences are in italics)

1940s

W.H. AUDEN: *New Year Letter*; 'In Praise of Limestone'.

ELIZABETH BISHOP: 'The Man-Moth'; 'Roosters'; 'The Fish'.

KEITH DOUGLAS: 'Cairo Jag'; 'Vergissmeinnicht'; 'How to Kill'.

T.S. ELIOT: 'East Coker'; 'The Dry Salvages'; 'Little Gidding'.

RANDALL JARRELL: 'Eighth Air Force'; 'The Death of the Ball Turret
  Gunner; 'Siegfried'; 'Second Air Force'; 'The Lines'.

PATRICK KAVANAGH: 'Shancoduff'; *The Great Hunger*; 'Epic'.

ALUN LEWIS: 'All Day It Has Rained'.

ROBERT LOWELL: 'The Quaker Graveyard in Nantucket'.

LOUIS MacNEICE: 'Prayer before Birth'.

HENRY REED: 'Lessons of the War'.

THEODORE ROETHKE: 'Dolor'; 'The Lost Son'.

DYLAN THOMAS: 'And Death Shall Have No Dominion'; 'A Refusal to
  Mourn the Death, by Fire, of a Child in London'; 'Fern Hill';
'Poem in October'.

R.S. THOMAS: 'A Peasant'.

1950s

W.H. AUDEN: 'The Shield of Achilles'; 'Goodbye to the Mezzogiorno'.

BASIL BUNTING: *The Spoils*.

ALLEN GINSBERG: *Howl*; *Kaddish*; 'A Supermarket in California'; 'America'

W.S. GRAHAM: *The Nightfishing*.

THOM GUNN: 'On the Move'.

TED HUGHES: 'Hawk Roosting'; 'View of a Pig'; 'Pike'

PHILIP LARKIN: 'Toads'; 'Church Going'; 'Mr Bleaney'; 'An Arundel
  Tomb'; 'The Whitsun Weddings'.

ROBERT LOWELL: 'Sailing Home from Rapallo'; 'Waking in the Blue';
  'Memories of West Street and Lepke'; 'Man and Wife'; 'To Speak
  of the Woe that is in Marriage'; 'Skunk Hour'.

EDWIN MUIR: 'The Horses'.

FRANK O'HARA: 'The Day Lady Died'.

W.D. SNODGRASS: *Heart's Needle*.

DYLAN THOMAS: 'Do Not Go Gentle into That Good Night'.

R.S. THOMAS: 'Evans'; 'A Welsh Testament'; 'Iago Prytherch'.

1960s

MARTIN BELL: 'Ode to Groucho'; 'Reasons for Refusal'.

JOHN BERRYMAN: *The Dream Songs*.

BASIL BUNTING: *Briggflatts*.

DOUGLAS DUNN: 'A Removal from Terry Street'; 'The Patricians'.

TONY HARRISON: 'The Nuptial Torches'; 'Newcastle Is Peru'.

SEAMUS HEANEY: 'Death of a Naturalist'; 'Digging'; 'Personal Helicon'.

GEOFFREY HILL: 'Ovid in the Third Reich'; 'September Song'.

TED HUGHES: *Crow*.

RANDALL JARRELL: 'The Lost World'; 'Thinking of the Lost World'.

PHILIP LARKIN: 'Here'; 'Dockery and Son'; 'High Windows'; 'Annus Mirabilis'.

MICHAEL LONGLEY: 'Letters'; 'Wounds'.

ROBERT LOWELL: 'For the Union Dead'; 'Waking Early Sunday Morning'.

ADRIAN MITCHELL: 'To Whom It May Concern (Tell me lies about Vietnam)'; 'Fifteen Million Plastic Bags'.

SYLVIA PLATH: 'Daddy'; 'Lady Lazarus'.

PETER PORTER: 'Your Attention Please'.

ANNE SEXTON: 'For My Lover, Returning to his Wife'.

JAMES WRIGHT: 'Lying in a Hammock at William Duffy's Farm…'

1970s

DOUGLAS DUNN: 'St Kilda's Parliament'; 'Washing the Coins'.

D.J. ENRIGHT: *The Terrible Shears.*

JAMES FENTON: 'A German Requiem'; 'A Staffordshire Murderer'; 'The Skip'; 'Cambodia'.

TONY HARRISON: 'Them & [uz]'; 'Book Ends'; 'Next Door'.

SEAMUS HEANEY: 'The Tollund Man'; *Singing School*; 'The Toome Road'; 'The Skunk';

LINTON KWESI JOHNSON: 'Five Nights of Bleeding'; 'Sonny's Lettah'.

PHILIP LARKIN: 'The Explosion'; 'This Be The Verse'

MICHAEL LONGLEY: 'Wreaths'; 'Peace'; 'The Linen Industry'.

DEREK MAHON: 'A Disused Shed in Co. Wexford'.

JOHN MONTAGUE: *The Rough Field.*

PETER PORTER: 'An Exequy'.

CRAIG RAINE: 'A Martian Sends a Postcard Home'.

KIT WRIGHT: 'Elizabeth'.

1980s

KAMAU BRATHWAITE: 'Stone'.

TONY CONRAN: 'Elegy for the Welsh Dead, in the Falkland Islands, 1982'.

PETER DIDSBURY: 'In Britain'; 'The Drainage'; 'Eikon Basilike'.

CAROL ANN DUFFY: 'Education for Leisure'; 'Weasel Words'.

DOUGLAS DUNN: *Europa's Lover*; 'Reading Pascal in the Lowlands'.

THOM GUNN: 'The Man with Night Sweats'; 'The Missing'.

TONY HARRISON: 'Continuous'; 'Timer'; 'Marked with D'; 'A Kumquat for John Keats'; 'The Fire-Gap'; 'v.'.

SEAMUS HEANEY: *Station Island*; 'From the Republic of Conscience'.

SELIMA HILL: *The Accumulation of Small Acts of Kindness.*

LINTON KWESI JOHNSON: 'Di Great Insohreckshan'.

BLAKE MORRISON: 'The Ballad of the Yorkshire Ripper'.

SEAN O'BRIEN: 'Cousin Coat'; 'London Road'; 'The Police'.

KEN SMITH: *Fox Running.*

1990s

TONY HARRISON: 'A Cold Coming'; 'Initial Illumination'.

JO SHAPCOTT: 'Phrase Book'.

CHAPTER FIFTEEN

Listings

ORGANISATIONS

Arts Councils

Literature Director
Arts Council of England
14 Great Peter Street
London SW1P 3NQ
☎ 0171-333 0100 FAX 0171-973 6590

Literature Director
Scottish Arts Council
12 Manor Place
Edinburgh EH3 7DD
☎ 0131-226 6051 FAX 0131-225 9833

Literature Director
**Arts Council of Wales/
Cyngor Celfyddydau Cymru**
9 Museum Place
Cardiff CF1 3NX
☎ 01222-394711 FAX 01222-221447

Literature Officer
**The Arts Council/
An Chomhairle Ealáion**
70 Merrion Square
Dublin 2
Eire
☎ 01-6611840 FAX 01-761302

Literature Director
Arts Council of Northern Ireland
185 Stranmillis Road
Belfast BT9 5DU
Northern Ireland
☎ 01232-381591 FAX 01232-661715

Regional Arts Boards/Associations

Northern Arts Board
9-10 Osborne Terrace
Newcastle upon Tyne NE2 1NZ
☎ 0191-2816334 FAX 0191-2813276
Area covered: Cleveland, Cumbria,
Durham, Northumberland, Tyne &
Wear.

**Yorkshire and Humberside
Arts Board**
21 Bond Street,
Dewsbury,
West Yorkshire WF13 1AX.
☎ 01924-455555 FAX 01924-466522
Area covered: North, South and West
Yorkshire, Humberside.

North West Arts Board
12 Harter Street
Manchester M1 6HY
☎ 0161-2283062 FAX 0161-2365361
Area covered: Greater Manchester,
High Peak District of Derbyshire,
Lancashire, Cheshire, Merseyside.

West Midlands Regional Arts Board
82 Granville Street
Birmingham B1 2LH
☎ 0121-6313121 FAX 0121-6437239
Area covered: Hereford & Worcester,
West Midlands, Shropshire, Staffordshire, Warwickshire.

East Midlands Arts Board
Mountfields House
Forest Road
Loughborough LE11 3HU
☎ 01509-218292 FAX 01509-262214
Area covered: Derbyshire, Notts,
Leicestershire, Northamptonshire.

Eastern Arts Board
Cherry Hinton Hall
Cherry Hinton Road
Cambridge CB1 4DW
☎ 01223-215355 FAX 01223-248075

Area covered: Cambridgeshire, Essex, Hertfordshire, Norfolk, Suffolk, Lincolnshire.

London Arts Board
Elme House
133 Long Acre, Covent Garden
London WC2E 9AF
☎ 0171-2401313 FAX 0171-2404580
Area covered: Greater London.

South East Arts Board
10 Mount Ephraim
Tunbridge Wells, Kent TN4 8AS
☎ 01892-515210 FAX 01892-549383
Area covered: Kent, Surrey, East Sussex.

Southern Arts Board
13 St Clement Street
Winchester, Hampshire SO23 9DQ
☎ 01962-855099 FAX 01962-861186
Area covered: Berkshire, Hampshire, Isle of Wight, Oxfordshire, West Sussex, Wiltshire, and Districts of Bournemouth, Christchurch & Poole.

South West Arts
Bradninch Place
Gandy Street
Exeter, Devon EX4 3LS
☎ 01392-218188 FAX 01392-413554
Area covered: Avon, Cornwall, Devon, Dorset (except Districts of Bournemouth, Christchurch & Poole), Gloucestershire, Somerset.

North Wales Arts Association/ Cymbeithas Gelfyddyau Gogledd Cymru
10 Wellfield House
Bangor, Gwynedd LL57 1ER
☎ 01248-353248 FAX 01248-351077
Area covered: Clwyd, Gwynedd and District of Montgomery in the County of Powys.

West Wales Arts/ Celfyddydau Gorllewin Cymru
3 Red Street
Carmarthen, Dyfed SA31 1QL
☎ 01267-234248 FAX 01267-233084
Area covered: Dyfed, West Glamorgan.

South East Wales Arts Association/ Cymdeithas Gelfyddydau De-Ddwyrain Cymru
Victoria Street
Cwmbran, Gwent NP44 3YT
☎ 01633-875075 FAX 01633-875389
Area covered: South Glamorgan, Mid Glamorgan, Gwent, Districts of Radnor and Brecknock in Powys and Cardiff.

Literature development workers & animateurs

Check with your Regional Arts organisation, library service or local authority to find out who is currently in post.

LIBRARIES

The Poetry Library
Royal Festival Hall
South Bank Centre
London SE1 8XX
☎ 0171-921 0664/0943

The Scottish Poetry Library
Tweeddale Court
14 High Street
Edinburgh EH1 1TE
☎ 0131-557 2876

Poetry Ireland
The Austin Clarke Library
Upper Yard, Dublin Castle
Dublin 2, Eire
☎ 01-6714632

Northern Poetry Library
County Library
The Willows
Morpeth
Northumberland NE61 1TA
☎ 01670-512385

BOOKSHOPS

A selective list of specialist shops is available from: The Poetry Library, Royal Festival Hall, South Bank Centre, London SE1 8XX.

POETRY, LITERATURE & WRITERS' ORGANISATIONS

The Poetry Society
22 Betterton Street
Covent Garden
London WC2H 9BU
☎ 0171-2404810 FAX 0171-2404818

The Poetry Book Society
Book House
45 East Hill
London SW18 2QZ
☎ 0181-8708403 FAX 081-8771615

Poetry Ireland
The Austin Clarke Library
Upper Yard
Dublin Castle
Dublin 2
Eire
☎ 01-6714632

**The Welsh Academy/
Yr Academi Gymreig**
3rd Floor
Mount Stuart House
Mount Stuart Square
Cardiff CF1 6DQ
☎ 01222-492025

Book Trust
Book House
45 East Hill
London SW18 2QZ
☎ 0181-8709055

Scottish Book Centre
137 Dundee Street
Edinburgh EH11 1BG
☎ 0131-2293663

Association of Little Presses
30 Greenhill
Hampstead High Street
London NW3 5UA
☎ 0171-435 1889

Small Press Group
BM Bozo
London WC1N 3XX
☎ 01234-211606

National Small Press Centre
(for *Small Press Listings*)
Middlesex University
White Hart Lane
London N17 8HR
☎ 0181-3626058

The Society of Authors
84 Drayton Gardens
London SW10 9SB
☎ 0171-3736642

Writers' Guild of Great Britain
430 Edgware Road
London W2 1EH
☎ 0171-723 8074/5/6

Authors' Guild of Ireland Ltd
282 Swords Road
Dublin 9,
Ireland
☎ 01-375974

Welsh Union of Writers
13 Richmond Road, Roath
Cardiff CF2 3AQ
☎ 01222-490303

**The Federation of Worker Writers
and Community Publishers**
68 Grand Parade
Brighton BN2 2JY

The Society of Women Writers
110 Whitehall Road
Chingford
London E4 6DW

**Commonword Ltd
(Cultureword Inc)**
c/o 21 Newton Street
Cheetwood House
Manchester M1 12F
☎ 0161-236 2773

National Poetry Foundation
27 Mill Road
Fareham,
Hampshire PO16 0TH
☎ 01329-822218

British Haiku Society
27 Park Street
Westcliff-on-Sea
Essex SS0 7PA

CRITICAL SERVICES

Many Regional Arts organisations offer excellent critical services free or at a very reasonable cost. Others include:

The Script
Poetry Society
22 Betterton Street
Covent Garden
London WC2H 9BU

Poetry Ireland Critical Service
The Austin Clarke Library
Upper Yard
Dublin Castle
Dublin 2
Eire

School of Poets Critical Service
Scottish Poetry Library
Tweeddale Court
14 High Street
Edinburgh EH1 1TE

Arts Council of Wales Critical Service
9 Museum Place
Cardiff CF1 3NX

WRITING COURSES

The Arvon Foundation
Totleigh Barton
Sheepwash
Beaworthy
Devon EX21 5NS
☎ 01409-231338

The Arvon Foundation
Lumb Bank
Heptonstall
Hebden Bridge
West Yorkshire HX7 6DF
☎ 01422-843714

The Arvon Foundation
Moniack Mhor
Kiltarlity
Beauly
Inverness-shire IV4 7HT
☎ 01463-741675

The Taliesin Trust
Tŷ Newydd
Llanystumdwy
Cricieth
Gwynedd LL52 0LW
☎ 01766-522811

Loch Ryan Writers
Loch Ryan Hotel
119 Sidbury
Worcester WR5 2DH
☎ 01905-351143

The Hen House
(*women's courses*)
North Thoresby
Lincs DN36 5QL

Denehurst Writers' Centre
Alford Road
Mablethorpe
Lincs LN12 1PX

The Poet's House
James & Janice Fitzpatrick Simmons
80 Portmuck Road
Island Magee
Co. Antrim
Northern Ireland
☎ 019603-82646

Fen Farm Writing Courses
10 Angel Hill
Bury St Edmunds
Suffolk IP33 1UZ
☎ 01379-898741 *or* 01284-753110

Old Hall
Margaret Steward & Peter Scupham
South Burlingham
Norwich NR13 4EY
☎ 01493-750804

The Poetry Business
The Studio
Byram Arcade
Huddersfield HD1 1ND
☎ 01484-434840

MAGAZINES & PERIODICALS

These are a few of the magazines that publish poetry. Most are specialist poetry magazines, but this list also includes general interest cultural and literary periodicals which publish some poetry. Updated lists can be obtained from The Poetry Library, South Bank Centre, London SE1 8XX (send an s.a.e.). A fuller list appears in *Small Presses and Little Magazines of the UK & Ireland* from Oriel Bookshop, The Friary, Cardiff CF1 4AA (£2.50). Many Regional Arts organisations publish stimulating magazines for writers which put you in touch with the local scene. Most magazines have a particular specialisation or favour certain kinds of poetry; if you send work to a magazine you have not read, you should not be surprised to have it rejected. The key to success in getting your work published is reading and proper research of likely outlets.

ENGLAND:

Acumen
6 The Mount
Higher Furzeham
Brixham, Devon TQ5 8QY

Agenda
5 Cranbourne Court
Albert Bridge Road
London SW11 4PE

Ambit
17 Priory Gardens
London N6 5QY

Angel Exhaust
c/o 27 Sturton Street
Cambridge CB1 2QG

Bête Noire
Department of American Studies
The University
Cottingham Road
Hull HU6 7RX

Critical Quarterly
Basil Blackwell Ltd
108 Cowley Road
Oxford OX4 1JF

Envoi
44 Rudyard Road
Biddulph Moor
Stoke-on-Trent ST8 7JN

Foolscap
78 Friars Road
East Ham
London E6 1LL

The Frogmore Papers
42 Morehall Avenue
Folkestone
Kent CT19 4EF

The Haiku Quarterly
39 Exmouth Street
Swindon SN1 3PU

Hybrid
42 Christchurch Place
Peterlee
Co. Durham SR8 2NR

Iron
5 Marden Terrace
Cullercoats
North Shields NE30 4PD

The Literary Review
51 Beak Street
London W1R 3LF

London Magazine
30 Thurloe Place
London SW7 2HQ

London Review of Books
28-30 Little Russell Street
London WC1A 2HN

New Statesman & Society
Foundation House
Perseverance Works
38 Kingsland Road
London E2 8DQ

The North
The Poetry Business
The Studio
Byram Arcade
Westgate
Huddersfield HD1 1ND

Orbis
199 The Long Shoot
Nuneaton CV11 6JQ

Outposts
22 Whitewell Road
Frome
Somerset BA11 4EL

Oxford Poetry
Magdalen College
Oxford OX1 4AU

PN Review
208-212 Corn Exchange
Manchester M4 3BQ

Pennine Platform
Ingmanthorpe Hall Farm Cottage
Wetherby
West Yorkshire LS22 5EQ

Poetry London Newsletter
Golden Cockerel Press
16 Barter Street
London WC1A 2AH

Poetry Review
The Poetry Society
22 Betterton Street
London WC2H 9BU

Poetry Quarterly Review
Coleridge Cottage
Nether Stowey
Somerset TA5 1NQ

The Printer's Devil
Top Office,
13A Western Road,
Hove,
East Sussex BN3 1AE.

The Rialto
32 Grosvenor Road
Norwich NR2 2PZ

Scratch
9 Chestnut Road
Eaglescliffe
Stockton-on-Tees TS16 0BA

Smiths Knoll
Goldings
Goldings Lane
Suffolk IP16 4EB

Smoke
Windows Project
40 Canning Street
Liverpool L8 7NP

Southfields
98 Gressenhall Road
Southfields
London SW18 5QJ

Stand
179 Wingrove Road
Newcastle upon Tyne NE4 9DA

Staple
School of Humanities
Derbyshire College of H.E.
Mickleover DE3 5GX

Sunk Island Review
P.O. Box 74
Lincoln LN1 1QG

Tears in the Fence
38 Hod View
Stourpaine, Blandford Forum
Dorset DT11 8TN

Thumbscrew
P.O. Box 657
Oxford OX2 6PH

Times Literary Supplement
Admiral House
66-68 East Smithfield
London E1 9XX

Wasafiri
P.O. Box 195
Canterbury CT2 7XB

Westwords
15 Trelawney Road
Peverell
Plymouth PL3 4JS

The Wide Skirt
1A Church Street
Penistone
South Yorkshire S30 6AR

Writing Women
Hawthorn House
Forth Banks
Newcastle upon Tyne NE1 3SG

SCOTLAND

Cencrastus
Unit One, Abbeymount Techbase
8 Easter Place
Edinburgh EH8 8EJ

Chapman
4 Broughton Place
Edinburgh EH1 3RX

Gairfish
71 Long Lane
Dundee DD5 2AS

Gairm
29 Waterloo Street
Glasgow G2 6BZ

Lines Review
Tweeddale Court
14 High Street
Edinburgh EH1 1TE

Northlight
136 Byres Road
Glasgow G12 8TD

WALES

The New Welsh Review
Gymnasium Building
UCW Cardiff
49 Park Place,
Cardiff CF1 3AT

Planet: The Welsh Internationalist
P.O. Box 44, Aberystwyth,
Dyfed SY24 5BS

Poetry Wales
Glan-y-Werydd
Llandanwg, Harlech
Gwynedd LL46 2SD

IRELAND

Bullán
42 George Street
Cambridge CB1 1AJ

Cyphers
3 Selskar Terrace
Dublin 6
Eire

Fortnight
7 Lower Crescent
Belfast BT7 1NR
Northern Ireland

Graph
34 Bellevue Park Avenue
Booterstown
Co. Dublin
Eire

Gown
75 Portmuck Road
Islandmagee
Northern Ireland

The Honest Ulsterman
14 Shaw Street
Belfast BT4 1PT
Northern Ireland

Krino
P.O. Box 65
Dún Laoghaire
Co. Dublin
Eire

Poetry Ireland Review
Upper Yard
Dublin Castle
Dublin 2
Eire

PUBLISHERS

A selective list. There are more main-stream publishers who have poets on their lists, but some do not take on new poets. There are many more small presses which are listed in *Small Presses and Little Magazines of the UK and Ireland*. A number of poetry presses are represented by: Password (Books) Ltd, 23 New Mount Street, Manchester M4 4DE. Most poetry publishers and small presses favour certain kinds of poetry. Do not submit a book to publishers unless you're familiar with and respect the poetry they already publish, otherwise you're wasting your time and theirs. As with magazines, the key to success in getting a book published is reading and proper research into imprints likely to be interested in your work; try getting poems into magazines first, and don't be impatient to get your book published (if your submission is premature – *and most are* – it will be rejected).

Publishers with poetry lists:

Blackstaff Press
3 Galway Park, Dundonald
Northern Ireland BT16 0AN

Jonathan Cape
Random Century House
20 Vauxhall Bridge Road
London SW1V 2SA

Faber & Faber
3 Queen Square
London WC1N 3AU

Harvill Press
84 Thornhill Road
London N1 1RD

Oxford University Press
Walton Street
Oxford OX2 6DP

Penguin/Viking
27 Wright's Lane
London W8 5TZ

Specialist poetry publishers
Some of these also publish other kinds of books, usually in related areas such as literature, literary criticism, drama and fiction.

Anvil Press Poetry
69 King George Street
London SE10 8PX

Arc Publications
(formerly Littlewood Arc)
The Nanholme Centre
Shaw Wood Road
Todmorden OL14 6DA

Bloodaxe Books
PO Box 1SN
Newcastle upon Tyne NE99 1SN

Carcanet Press
208 Corn Exchange Buildings
Manchester M4 3BQ

Dedalus Press
24 The Heath
Cypress Downs
Dublin 6W
Eire

Enitharmon Press
36 St George's Avenue
London N7 0HD

Flambard Press
4 Mitchell Avenue
Jesmond
Newcastle upon Tyne NE2 3LA

Gallery Press
Loughcrew
Oldcastle
Co. Meath
Eire

Peterloo Poets
2 Kelly Gardens
Calstock
Cornwall PL18 9SA

Salmon Publishing
Knockeven
Cliffs of Moher
Co. Clare
Eire

Seren Books
(*formerly Poetry Wales Press*)
First Floor, Wyndham Street
Bridgend
Mid Glamorgan CF31 1EF

Smaller Poetry Presses

Allardyce Barnett
14 Mount Street
Lewes, East Sussex BN7 1HL.

Headland Publications
38 York Avenue, West Kirby
Wirral L48 3JF

Hippopotamus Press
22 Whitewell Road
Frome,
Somerset BA11 4EL

Iron Press
5 Marden Terrace
Cullercoats
North Shields NE30 4PD

Pig Press
7 Cross View Terrace
Neville's Cross
Durham DH1 4JY

Rockingham Press
11 Musley Lane
Ware, Herts SG12 7EN

Scratch
9 Chestnut Avenue
Eaglescliffe
Stockton-on-Tees TS16 0BA

Smith/Doorstop Books
The Poetry Business
The Studio, Byram Arcade
Huddersfield HD1 1ND

Stride Publications/Taxus Press
11 Sylvan Road
Exeter EX4 6EW

University of Salzburg Press
Institut für Anglistik und Amerikanistik
Universität Salzburg
Akademiestrasse 24
A-5020 Salzburg, Austria
(Distributor: Hippopotamus Press)

Wellsweep Press
(*Oriental poetry in translation*)
1 Grove End House
150 Highgate Road
London NW5 1PD

Black Presses

Dangaroo Press
(*post-colonial and women's poetry*)
P.O. Box 20
Hebden Bridge
West Yorkshire HX7 5UZ

New Beacon Books
76 Stroud Green Road
London N4 3EN

Peepal Tree Press
17 Kings Avenue
Leeds LS6 1QS

Race Today
165 Railton Road
London SE24 0LU

Women's Presses

Onlywomen Press
40 St Lawrence Terrace
London W10 5ST

Virago Press
Brettenham House
Lancaster Place
London WC2E 7EH

The Women's Press
34 Great Sutton Street
London EC1V 0DX

Gay Presses

GMP Publishers
(Gay Men's Press)
PO Box 247
London N15 6RW

Oscars Press
BM Oscars
London WC1N 3XX

REFERENCE BOOKS

Writers' & Artists' Yearbook: A & C Black (annual).

Small Presses & Little Magazines of the UK and Ireland: Oriel Bookshop, The Friary, Cardiff CF1 4AA (£2.50 inc p&p).

The Writer's Handbook: Papermac.

Writing in Wales: Welsh Academy resource pack.

Jessie Lendennie & Paddy Hickson: *The Salmon Guide to Creative Writing in Ireland:* Salmon Publishing Co.

Gerald Dawe: *How's the Poetry Going?: Literary Politics and Ireland Today:* Lagan Press, 7 Lower Crescent, Belfast BT7 1NR.

Peter Finch: *How to Publish Your Poetry:* Allison & Busby (1985).

Peter Finch: *How to Publish Yourself:* Allison & Busby (1988).

Peter Finch: *The Poetry Business:* Seren (1994).

Evangeline Paterson: *What to do with your poems:* Other Poetry Editions, 8 Oakhurst Tce, Benton, Newcastle upon Tyne NE12 9NY (£3.45).

A Guide to Literary Prizes, Grants and Awards in Britain and Ireland: Book Trust (£3.75).

Directory of Writers' Circles: from Jill Dick, Oldacre, Horderns Park Road, Chapel-en-le-Frith, Derbyshire SK12 6SY.

Johnathon Clifford: *Vanity Press & the Proper Poetry Publishers:* Johnathon Clifford

Peter Sansom: *Writing Poems:* Bloodaxe Books.

Michael Baldwin: *The Way to Write Poetry:* Elm Tree Books.

John Fairfax & John Moat: *The Way to Write:* Elm Tree Books.

Dorothea Brande: *Becoming a Writer:* Papermac.

Gillian Allnutt: *Berthing: A Poetry Workbook:* NEC/Virago.

Judson Jerome: *The Poet's Handbook:* Writer's Digest Books.

G.S. Fraser: *Metre, Rhyme and Free Verse:* Methuen.

Ted Hughes: *Poetry in the Making:* Faber.

Robin Skelton: *The Practice of Poetry:* Heinemann.

Philip Davies Roberts: *How Poetry Works:* Penguin.

Graham Martin & P.N. Furbank: *Twentieth-Century Poetry: Critical Essays and Documents:* Open University Press.

Alex Preminger: *Princeton Encyclopedia of Poetry and Poetics:* Princeton.

James Scully: *Modern Poets on Modern Poetry:* Fontana.

George Plimpton: *Poets at Work: Paris Review Interviews:* 5 vols, Penguin.

Tracy Chevalier: *Contemporary Poets,* 5th edition: St James Press.

Ian Hamilton: *Oxford Companion to Twentieth Century Poetry in English:* Oxford University Press.

Jonathan Barker: *Poetry in Britain since 1970: A select bibliography:* British Council.

Ezra Pound: *ABC of Reading:* Faber.

Vernon Scannell: *How to Enjoy Poetry:* Piatkus.

Frances Stillman: *The Poet's Manual and Rhyming Dictionary:* Thames & Hudson

BLOODAXE POETRY HANDBOOKS: 2
Writing Poems
by PETER SANSOM

Drawing on his extensive experience of poetry workshops and courses, Peter Sansom shows you not how to write but how to write better, how to write authentically, how to say genuinely what you genuinely mean to say. This practical guide is illustrated with many examples.

Peter Sansom covers such areas as submitting to magazines; the small presses; analysing poems; writing techniques and procedures; and drafting. He includes brief resumés and discussions of literary history and literary fashions, the spirit of the age, and the creative process itself. Above all, his book helps you learn discrimination in your reading and writing – so that you can decide for yourself how you want your work to develop, whether that magazine was right in returning it or if they simply don't know their poetic arse from their elbow.

WRITING POEMS includes sections on:
- Metre, rhyme, half-rhyme and free verse.
- Fixed forms and how to use them.
- Workshops and writing groups.
- Writing games and exercises.
- A detailed, annotated reading list.
- Where to go from here.
- Glossary of technical terms.

Peter Sansom is a leading contemporary poet. His books include *On the Pennine Way* (Littlewood, 1988) and two collections from Carcanet, *Everything You've Heard Is True* (1990), a Poetry Book Society Recommendation, and *January* (1994). He has held several placements in schools and colleges and has also worked extensively with teachers. For three years he was writer-in-residence at Doncaster Central Library. He is a director of The Poetry Business in Huddersfield, and co-editor of *The North* Magazine and Smith/Doorstop Books and Cassettes.

Paperback £7.95   128 pages   ISBN 1 85224 204 3